ANCESTRY DAILY NEWS

COLLECTOR'S EDITION • MAY 2002

ANCESTRY DAILY NEWS

COLLECTOR'S EDITION • MAY 2002

EDITED BY JULIANA S. SMITH

Ancestry.

Table of Contents

Editor's Note

As FAMILY HISTORIANS WE FIND OURSELVES RUNNING from place to place, surfing the Net, e-mailing, snail-mailing, and faxing—all this to collect every record we can get our hands on for our ancestors. These documents are noted and then filed away as we go off in search of more records. Every so often it's a good idea to go back and take a look at what we've accumulated (which can sometimes be an intimidating task!). Besides collecting these documents, we need to cull every little piece of information from them and analyze them as we work to bring the lives of our ancestors into focus.

Analyzing records seemed to be the prevailing theme for many of May's *Ancestry Daily News* articles. Michael provides studies of both vital and census records, as well as resolving conflicting information, and Pat Hatcher took a look at some "Likely and Unlikely Mistakes." In my own column, I take a look at analyzing "What the Records Don't Say."

In other articles, Sherry takes a good look at Pallot's Indexes to births and marriages in England, Pat spills "The Secret That Professionals Don't Share," and George G. Morgan talks about everything from Personal Digital Assistants (PDAs) to "Planning Your Family Reunion." Karen Frisch talks about "Naming Customs," and in honor of Memorial Day, Megan Smolenyak tells us about a remarkable project started by a remarkable man named Andrew Carroll.

May 2002

There are, of course, more articles, and the usual great selection of Quick Tips, but I'm guessing by now you're ready to dive into this issue. I hope you enjoy it!

Best of luck with your search!
Juliana Smith

Contributors

Karen Frisch has spent years getting lost in cemeteries. With a background in Victorian studies, teaching, and writing, she has traced her lineage back thirty generations. Her interest in genealogy began as a child when her grandmother gave her a collection of old photographs from Scotland.

Patricia Law Hatcher, CG^{sm}, FASG, is a technical writer, instructor, and professional genealogist. Her oft-migrating ancestors lived in all of the original colonies prior to 1800 and in seventeen other states, presenting her with highly varied research problems and forcing her to acquire techniques and tools that help solve tough problems. She is the author of *Producing a Quality Family History*.

Sherry Irvine, CGRS^{sm}, FSA(Scot) is an author, teacher, and lecturer specializing in English and Scottish family history. She is the author of *Your English Ancestry* (2nd ed, 1998) and *Your Scottish Ancestry* (1997) and a regular contributor to several journals including *Genealogical Computing*. Since 1996 she has been a study tour leader, course coordinator, and instructor for the Institute of

Genealogy and Historical Research, Samford University. She teaches online for the family history program of Vermont College and has lectured at conferences in Canada, the United States, and Australia. She is president of the Association of Professional Genealogists.

George G. Morgan is the president of Tampa-based Aha! Seminars, Inc., which is engaged in continuing education for libraries across Florida and the Southeast. He also is an internationally recognized genealogist. He is the author of three online columns, two books, two compilations, and magazine and journal articles published in the U.S., Canada, and the U.K. He is a frequent speaker at genealogical societies, at genealogy conferences, and is the Program Chair for the 2003 Federation of Genealogical Societies Conference to be held in Orlando, Florida, in September next year.

Michael John Neill, is the Course I Coordinator at the Genealogical Institute of Mid America (GIMA) held annually in Springfield, Illinois, and is on the faculty of Carl Sandburg College in Galesburg, Illinois. Michael is the Web columnist for the FGS *FORUM* and is on the editorial board of the Illinois State Genealogical Society *Quarterly*. He conducts seminars and lectures on a wide variety of genealogical and computer topics and contributes to several genealogical publications, including *Ancestry* and *Genealogical Computing*.

Juliana S. Smith has been the editor of the *Ancestry Daily News* and *Weekly Digest* since 1998. She is also the author of *The Ancestry Family Historian's Address Book* and has written for *Ancestry* Magazine and *Genealogical Computing*. Juliana works from her home in Indiana where she lives with her husband, six-year-old daughter, dog, and two cats. In her spare time, she enjoys chasing down her own ancestors.

Megan Smolenyak, author of *Honoring Our Ancestors: Inspiring Stories of the Quest for Our Roots* and *In Search of Our Ancestors: 101 Inspiring Stories of Serendipity and Connection in Rediscovering Our*

Family History, was the lead researcher for the PBS *Ancestors* series and the forthcoming *They Came to America*. She supports innovative genealogical initiatives through her Honoring Our Ancestors Grants Program and can be reached through her website at <www.honoringourancestors.com>.

Esther H. Yu is the associate editor of the *Ancestry Daily News* and *Weekly Digest*. She is a contributing editor for *Ancestry* Magazine and writes the Community section in each issue of the magazine. She recently unearthed many old family photographs, which has led to new and exciting details about her ancestry and life in her ancestral homeland, Taiwan.

"To be ignorant of what occurred before you were born is to remain always a child. For what is the worth of human life, unless it is woven into the life of our ancestors by the records of history?"

—*Marcus Tullius Cicero, 106-43 B.*

Family History Compass

Fight "Research Frenzy" with a Search Strategy
May 6, 2002
Juliana Smith

I JUST FOUND OUT THAT IN JUNE, I'll be making a trip to Utah to visit the Ancestry.com home offices. While there, I plan to take a few extra days to do some research in the Family History Library (FHL) in Salt Lake City. (Commence happy dancing!)

In order to get the most from my trip, I need to get my ducks in a row now, so that when I go, I have a solid research plan. Without a plan, I run the risk of duplicating work that I've already done, wasting precious FHL time searching records I could access anytime—from either local repositories or on the Internet—and even searching the wrong records. Since this is a relatively rare opportunity for me, I want to make sure I take full advantage of the unique collections that await me in Salt Lake City!

One of the first things I'm going to do is go over my research and fill in any holes that I can from home or local repositories.

There are a number of new databases at Ancestry.com that I haven't had time to really search, and that may give me some answers. I also still have a few elusive ancestors that absolutely refuse to be found in the census, despite numerous attempts. I'm determined to give it another try, and using some creative approaches to searching, I hope to fill in these gaps before my trip.

My trouble is, I get into a "search frenzy" of sorts, and just start plugging in name after name, using as many variants as I can think of, adding in and leaving out various criteria, performing wildcard searches, Soundex searches, and trying all of these in different locations. After a while, my head is spinning and I can't remember where I've searched for what names, and how. Did I miss something?

When I go to a library, I'm really good about recording what films I have searched, books I have checked, etc., in a log so that when I go back, I don't come home with the same findings I did a few months back. Since I am the mother of a six-year-old who has her own agenda when we're in the library, my research time is precious stuff!

But for some reason when I'm sitting at my computer in my jammies, I tend to overlook this step. I have probably wasted countless hours sitting here re-searching the same indexes over and over, while I still have no idea whether or not I've done a comprehensive search.

Resolution time! I am about to embark on a new phase in my at-home research and begin treating it like I would a trip to the library. After all, I often have to make trade-offs here to get in research time. Since this often means giving up much-needed hours of sleep to do "just a few more searches," isn't my research time here valuable, too?

So here goes . . .

(Raise my right hand) "I, Juliana Smith, hereby resolve to form a solid research plan before attacking the keyboard, and keep track of my frenzied searches online."

So How Do I Keep My Resolution?

To start with, I'm going to take Pat Hatcher's advice from her column of last Thursday, and write a research report (See <http://www.ancestry.com/rd/prodredir.asp?sourceid=831&key=A

56930> for more on this.) Since I already have a timeline that includes source information, it shouldn't be too difficult. Writing out the problem, the documented facts I have, and analyzing conclusions drawn from these facts, I'll have a clearer picture of where I want to start. I am making this the first page in a "case file" I have created for this problem.

Using a spreadsheet to keep track of my searches, I am ready to head back into the census indexes to see if I can at last locate the family I am seeking in the 1850 and 1860 censuses. I have created fields on the spreadsheet for the various criteria that I can enter in the advanced search template and added a few fields of my own so that the headers on the page read:

- Given name
- Surname
- Soundex code
- Soundex On?
- State
- County
- District
- Pages Viewed
- Keyword
- Proximity
- Results Page #

"District" and "Pages Viewed" are for cases where I do a page-by-page search of a census district. The "Results Page #" field will reference the printed page of the relevant hits for that particular search. These prints are filed numerically and I make notes on them as I follow up and either rule them out or keep them as a possibility. We'll discuss the "Soundex Code" column later in the article.

How Many Searches Am I Planning?
With all of the other things I have on my plate right now, a page-by-page search of Brooklyn for those years is not a practical option (although it is certainly not out of the question for this obsessed family historian!). So I will rely first on indexes and get creative

with my searches to see what I can find first. Here are some things I'll look for:

- **Dropped and Similar Sounding Letters**

  I have been tutoring kindergartners in my daughter's class over the last couple of weeks, working on spelling out words by stretching them out and listening for the letter sounds. As they work on journal entries, the children often misinterpret similar sounding letters as they write. Vowels are easy targets for this.

  In addition, the words and letters that don't have a strong sound or are silent are often dropped. An enumerator knocking at my ancestor's door could have made a similar mistake. (After all some of them wrote like kindergartners!) This has proved true in previous searches. After searching high and low for one ancestor, Thomas Howley, I finally found him enumerated as Thomas Holey. In another example, my third great-grandmother Ann Dwyer is listed as Toire, Ware, Wire, and Weir—all in the same book.

  I will no doubt draw strange looks from family and animals as I sit here stretching and sounding out the names I'm searching for, but if it works, it will be well worth it!

- **Soundex Searches**

  Many of the databases at Ancestry.com, including the census indexes, allow for Soundex searching. This feature will capture many misspellings resulting from similar sounds, but as the examples listed above for Ann Dwyer demonstrate, there will still be more that won't be caught, particularly when the similar sound is the first letter of the name. To help keep track of the Soundex variants I am searching, I use the "Soundex Code" column to list the code for each name searched. For more information on the Soundex Code, see the National Archives page at <http://www.nara.gov/genealogy/coding.html> or try a search in the Ancestry.com Library for "Soundex." A number of good articles are available there that can give further insight into the coding system.

- **Transposition Errors**

  Not all errors originated with the enumerator. Transpositions are commonly found in indexes and can also result in spellings that Soundex won't pick up. It's also important to remember that the transpositions don't always show up in last names. If you're including a given name, be aware that a misspelled first name can throw you off the track, too.

- **Abbreviations**

  How many times have you seen records listing Jas. for James, Wm. for William, Jos. for Joseph, Thos. for Thomas, Chas. for Charles or even just the initials. Databases typically can't interpret these abbreviations for us, so these are other variants to keep in mind.

- **Who's in Charge Here?**

  The other day I was searching for Harry Truman in the 1920 Census. (Yes, I'm truly sick. I even search for nonrelatives!) Searches for Harry Truman and several variants didn't turn him up in Independence, Missouri, where he was married in 1919 so I did a little digging on the Internet. The Truman Library site provided just what I needed with a map of "Truman Places" that gave addresses and biographical tidbits. A search for his mother-in-law's name, Madge Wallace, turned him up living in her household. This is a good reminder to check the households of in-laws and other family members who have a different surname. (Census subscribers can see Harry and Bess in Census Images Online by going to <http://www.ancestry.com/search/rectype/census/usfedcen/main.htm> and selecting 1920—Missouri—Jackson County—Other Townships—ED #7—Image 27 of 41.)

Comparing with Other Records

Since in this case, I have a baptism from 1834 in Brooklyn, and the next reference I have to the family is a marriage in 1865 in Brooklyn, the logical place to start searching in 1850 and 1860 is Brooklyn. But how do I know if I've caught everyone? I went to some directories for this time, and am doing a comparison of the individuals who share my ancestor's name in the directories, with those I found in the census. With the occupations listed and using a map to locate addresses in various districts, I am hoping to match up the entries. Any directory listings that I don't have census information for can be searched for manually by location.

In Closing
There are of course more things to consider when looking for variants, such as last name listed as first name, letters that look alike, etc., but as usual, this column has gone on too long. (Just call me motor-fingers!) So I'm going to leave you with this and hope that I've at least given you a few ideas for some of your searches. Good luck!!!

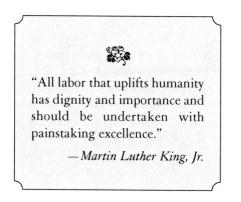

"All labor that uplifts humanity has dignity and importance and should be undertaken with painstaking excellence."
— *Martin Luther King, Jr.*

Clues in What Records Don't Say
13 May 2002
Juliana Smith

*O*NE OF THE MOST ADMIRABLE THINGS ABOUT HISTORY *is, that almost as a rule we get as much information out of what it does not say as we get out of what it does say. And so, one may truly and axiomatically aver this, to-wit: that history consists of two equal parts; one of these halves is statements of fact, the other half is inference, drawn from the facts. To the experienced student of history there are no difficulties about this; to him the half which is unwritten is as clearly and surely visible, by the help of scientific inference, as if it flashed and flamed in letters of fire before his eyes. When the practised eye of the simple peasant sees the half of a frog projecting above the water, he unerringly infers the half of the frog which he does not see. To the expert student in our great science, history is a frog; half of it is submerged, but he knows it is there, and he knows the shape of it."*

— Mark Twain, "The Secret History of Eddypus"

One of the fun parts of this job is going out and searching for good quotes to run as the "Thought for Today." When I ran across this one, I thought, "Wow, this is perfect!" But as I re-read it and thought about it in the context of my recent research efforts, I had to wonder about my "scientific prowess." I have really looked for those "flashed and flamed letters" before my eyes, but the only thing I see flashing before my eyes are stars from beating my head on brick walls.

Why Can't I See the Frog?

Well, if there's a frog anywhere in the vicinity of my desk, he's probably hiding under a pile of papers. (Yes, they still seem to reappear despite a valiant effort of late to keep my desk clean, but that's an article for another day.)

So I guess my first job is to find the part of the frog that's visible —in other words, assemble the facts as I know them. Sound familiar? Yes, you've heard me say it many times before in other columns. It's an important first step when confronting a problem, and on the bright side, it's an encouraging way to start. Once we see that we actually have a little information on a person, that brick wall doesn't seem quite so insurmountable.

As I assemble what I have, I go over time lines I've created, where I use facts gleaned from documents and assemble them in a chronological fashion. I also like to pull out the original sources of that information and pore over them in their entirety as well. Often, a close examination of the details found in many records can provide clues that aren't really spelled out as such.

For example, in the 1890 census, questions included the number of years the person had lived in this country, and their naturalization status. Unfortunately, most of that census was lost in a fire, so for most of us, the 1900 census is the first census in which we can find this information spelled out. But, using information found in other years, we can often narrow down the date of immigration using dates and places of birth of family members. Below is the 1850 U.S. Federal Census entry for my third great-grandfather William Huggins.

HIGGINS, William, age 44, Mason, born in Ireland
- Ann, age 33, born in Ireland
- Robert, age 13, born in Ireland
- Catherine, age 8, born in Ireland

From Catherine's age and birthplace, I can theorize that the family immigrated to the U.S. between:

- ca. 1841-42 (Catherine's birth in Ireland according to the census) and
- 31 July 1850 (the date the census was taken)

This still leaves quite a time frame to deal with, particularly since the records after 1846 are not indexed. By adding other records to this mix, I can narrow it down even further. From "St. Paul's Roman Catholic Church, Brooklyn, NY, Baptisms and Marriage Registers: The Irish Parish," (1) I found the following baptisms:

Anne Huggins, bapt. 26 May 1844, born 28 Apr 1844
James Huggan, 22 Feb 1846, born 13 Feb 1846
William Huggins, 11 July 1847, born 5 July 1847
Ann Higgins, 12 Nov 1848, born 30 Oct 1846
William Huggins, 13 Nov 1853, 31 Sept 31
Margaret Huggan, 13 Oct 1850, 2 Oct 1850
Mary Huggins, 17 May 1857, 8 May 1857

All of these entries list William Huggins as the father and Ann as the mother, although the spellings for her maiden name of Dwyer are a bit "creative" (Wire, Ware, Dwyer, Toire, and Weir). Given the first baptism at St. Paul's for Anne in May 1844, we can now narrow the immigration date down a bit further to between around 1842 and May 1844. And since this period of passenger lists through New York are indexed (yeah!), it will be worth it to take a look-see next time I'm at the National Archives.

Another clue I find that isn't exactly spelled out, is in the baptism registry. There are two Ann(e)s listed, and two Williams listed. Now either they have a household like George Foreman where all the kids have the same names, or the first Anne and William died before the later Ann and William. Looking for a death record is another option, and since the time frame the Municipal Archives specifies for a search is five years, I could get lucky.

The Frog Thickens

These examples were pretty simple ones, but as we go further back and records are more scarce and scant in details, we may find ourselves looking at cases that get quite a bit more complicated. Not only will we be looking at a variety of records to try to narrow down dates, but also to determine relationships and other things that later censuses spell out so nicely for us. In these cases, we're going to have to be a bit more careful. In the above examples, there are relatively simple follow-up steps we can take to confirm the theories we draw from records. This may not always be the case, and we may find ourselves analyzing and weighing the information found in any number of records, in order to form a solid conclusion.

Is It a Frog or a Toad?

Mark Twain is right on the money when he refers to history as a science. When drawing conclusions from records, it's very important that you approach it in scientific way, considering all the possibilities and variables, and cite the reasons for your conclusion. By making sure your research is sound, you can be reasonably sure you're tracing your family's frogs and not the toad family next door.

Regardless of how simple or complex the inferences you draw from records, it is also critical that you cite the reasons for your conclusions because:

- You may think that you'll remember it, but I have learned the hard way too many times that what seems an obvious conclusion at 1 a.m. (when most of my research seems to get done these days), is not nearly as obvious in the light of day, or months down the road when I pull that dusty binder off the shelf.

- If you decide to share your findings with others in the future, the course of your research will be documented, adding credibility to your work.

- When you commit your theories to paper, it becomes easier to see whether or not they will hold water. I can't tell you how many times I come upon amazing finds that I think will make wonderful articles. Yet, when I begin to write them down and explain my train of thought, the holes surface and they fall apart. There's no telling how much research time and money have been saved by writing this column!

That's it for this week. I'm off now in search of some frogs in my family tree that need dissecting. (Okay, maybe that's taking the metaphor a bit too far!)

References
1. "St. Paul's Roman Catholic Church, Brooklyn, New York, Baptisms and Marriage Registers: The Irish Parish" (Salt Lake City, Utah: Redmond Press, 1996).

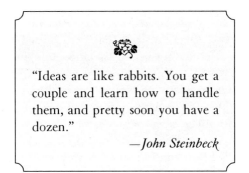

"Ideas are like rabbits. You get a couple and learn how to handle them, and pretty soon you have a dozen."
—*John Steinbeck*

Messages May Come and Go, But Archives Are Forever
May 20 2002
Juliana Smith

A s EDITOR OF THE *ANCESTRY DAILY NEWS*, I receive some interesting mail. Questions and comments come from around the world and all levels of genealogists (and some non-genealogists). Unfortunately, I often receive messages where it is obvious that little thought has gone into the composition of the e-mail. I guess that it is in part due to the instant gratification that we receive through this wonderful thing called technology.

It's stating the obvious to say that technology has been a great boon to family historians. It has put records from around the world into the comfort of our homes, where we can sit in our bunny slippers and explore them at our leisure. It makes available reference materials to help us find our way and learn new research techniques. And one of the greatest benefits is that it brings us together and allows us to bond with other obsessed genealogy fanatics at any time of day or night. Message boards and mailing lists allow us to exchange research and techniques, and commiserate over brick walls. When we're lucky, we can also share the joy of a find with others who won't think we're "a bit off" for spending so much time prying into the lives of people we've never seen or met.

These message boards and mailing lists are also susceptible to some of the same types of messages I see in my inbox, and without a doubt, one of the most frequent suggestions I have for a column is to address one or more problems that are related to these forums. So, in today's "Family History Compass," I'll use some questions based on examples from my editor's mail to illustrate a few ways we can improve the posts we make to these wonderful forums.

"I've been collecting rocks since I was a child and would like to learn more about them. Can you recommend a good book?"

Here's someone with a legitimate question, but who is most definitely barking up the wrong tree. Despite the fact that geology and genealogy sound similar, they are in truth miles apart. The only rocks I'm interested have writing on them and are sitting on my ancestors' graves!

Often, we see posts made on boards and lists where although they might not be so drastically off track as this person, could be redirected to a more appropriate place. It's important to look at the purpose of the forum to which you plan on directing your query.

The folks on the Mongolian mailing list will probably not be able to help you find your ancestors from Ouagadougou, regardless of how knowledgeable they are about genealogy, nor are they likely to be inclined to discuss it. Your message (and the 50,000 scathing e-mails that are sure to follow) will be doomed to live on in the archives of the mailing list in infamy, while your Ougadougouan ancestors remain in obscurity.

Be sure to check out the homepage or welcome message for lists you've joined. Not only will this give you important subscription information (how to subscribe, unsubscribe, and post), but it should also provide any guidelines as to what is appropriate to post on the list.

"Since I pay taxes and social security, why am I not listed in the SSDI?"

It is glaringly obvious that this person didn't do his or her homework before asking this question and hasn't taken the time to learn that SSDI stands for Social Security DEATH Index—"death" being the operative word here. It is assumed that the composer of this message is not yet dead, and if he is, I should probably ask him a question—if he's seen my ancestors, please have them contact me as well. I have some questions.

Before posting a question to a mailing list, it's a good idea to do a little homework yourself. While many folks are wonderfully generous when it comes to helping out, some may become a little tired of answering questions for people unwilling to do a little digging themselves. Many mailing list home pages have an FAQ and/or basic information on resources available for those researching the area of interest that is the list's focus. Check it out, do some searches, and if the list or board is archived, search the archives to see whether or not that particular question has been asked before. Doing so will help reduce clutter in the archives, and people will be more likely to continue to help if they are not overwhelmed by the same questions over and over again.

"I've lost my ancestors. I think they're in the Ukraine."

First of all, again, this request is misdirected. Although I'd love to help this person with his or her research, I have to scrape time from the "wee hours" just to work on my own research, and like many other columnists/editors, I simply don't have any time to chase other people's ancestors.

Even if I did want to help this person, I couldn't do a thing with this type of request, and nor would anyone on the Ukrainian mailing list. Posts should include the pertinent details about the ancestor being researched. If you have more than one ancestor in the particular area, it's best to post your questions one at a time, including appropriate subject lines that will get people's attention. A good example for a subject line would be:

FOODJABUNNY, Herbert A. 1821 - ca. 1877, ENG>NY>OH

This tells us "who" we are talking about, "when" he lived, and "where" he was. The body of the message should give us "what" we want to know about him, and if we have formed a theory, "why" we believe it to be true. A post like this covers the "five Ws" and will also be much more likely to catch the eye of other descendants or cousins of Mr. Foodjabunny.

Other items you may want to include would be places you've already searched for your answer so you don't get fifty people sending you to something that's already been done or somewhere you've already been.

At the same time, you don't want to overwhelm people with an "epic e-mail" full of bits of interesting trivia about the ancestors that are unrelated to the problem at hand. While this is great fodder for the family history, the folks on the list don't want to wade through it to get to the meat of the problem. A short, to-the-point post will achieve much better results.

More on the Archives
Mailing list archives can be wonderful tools and many people overlook the search feature that is available with most of them. If you've recently joined a list, you may want to check out the archives and do some searches for your ancestors' names. Not only is this a good way to hook up with others researching the same lines, but many people post transcriptions of records related to the list's interests, making these list archives, in essence, free databases.

One thing that's good to bear in mind: If you have a signature line listing the surnames you are researching, it's helpful to others doing searches to insert spaces or characters between the names that are not relevant to the post. For example, if your post is about Mr. Foodjabunny, you might change your signature line to read as such:

Researching FOODJABUNNY, P*E*R*S*N*I*C*K*E*T*Y, B*U*G*A*B*O*O, and S*M*I*T*H

This way anyone searching the archives will only pick up the surname relevant to that particular post and not all the posts you made regarding your Bugaboo ancestry. Since it's a bit of a pain to type this up each time, it's relatively easy to create subject lines for each of your lines ahead of time, and then just cut and paste the relevant one for each post.

And in the End . . .

Ancestry.com's "sister company," RootsWeb.com maintains over 24,000 mailing lists, most of which are archived. See <http://lists.rootsweb.com> for a complete list of what is available and to locate the archives for each list.

The Ancestry.com Message Boards <http://boards.ancestry.com> provide another great searchable forum for posting and searching for your ancestors. There are currently over 126,000 with over 9.7 million posts

Mailing lists can be wonderful tools, and when you put a little thought into the messages, you might be surprised at what you can find. Give it a try!

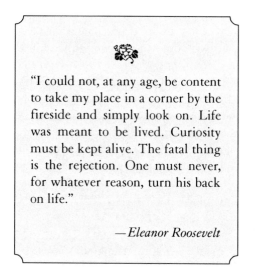

"I could not, at any age, be content to take my place in a corner by the fireside and simply look on. Life was meant to be lived. Curiosity must be kept alive. The fatal thing is the rejection. One must never, for whatever reason, turn his back on life."

— *Eleanor Roosevelt*

What Can We Do to Help Save Our Records?
38 May 2002
Juliana Smith

L AST WEEK THE *ANCESTRY DAILY NEWS* ran a Joint Resolution and Petition from the Federation of Genealogical Societies (FGS) and the National Genealogical Society (NGS) regarding the possible closure of California vital records indexes. (See <http://www.ancestry.com/rd/prodredir.asp?sourceid=831&key=A 577701>.)

I received a number of messages from readers asking what they could do to help. Because California legislators will be most likely to listen to their voters, it was particularly important that California residents write in to express their opinion.

The rest of us shouldn't be resting on our laurels though. Even if you don't have roots in California, this legislation sets a dangerous precedent and if it passes, other states may follow suit. In addition to vital records legislation, family historians are faced with other threats to record access, which include budget and staff cuts to the libraries and archives we rely on in researching our ancestry. So what can we do?

Be Proactive

Family historians are the principal users of our country's archives and as such, we are the first to be hurt when access and/or hours are restricted, and budgets are cut. Get to know your local librarians and archivists, learn about the challenges they face, and ask them what you can do as a patron to help.

There are volunteer programs both in the National Archives in Washington, DC, and in the regions. The volunteers have been responsible for a number of important preservation and education projects that might never have gotten off the ground had it been left to the bureaucrats. Volunteer networks help spread the word when records are being threatened and rally support to protect our national treasures.

Local libraries may have "friends" organizations that sponsor similar projects on a local level, like the Newberry Library's Friends of Genealogy (FOG), or Friends of the Allen County Public Library. Membership in these organizations help to fund special projects, acquisitions, expansions, and education, and also help support or voice displeasure over proposed legislation. Check your local libraries' websites and see what organizations support them.

The work of these dedicated people helps our libraries and archives stretch their budgets and do things that they might not otherwise be able to do. This benefits the community and its resident genealogists—like you!

Be Countable As a Society Member

One of the best ways (and the most fun!) is to join a society. When you are on a society membership list, you are countable as someone with an interest in family history. When legislation arises, these membership numbers can be used to exert influence over those we vote into (or out of) office.

In addition, there are many other wonderful benefits in belonging to a society. With your membership, you will typically receive periodicals, access to society holdings, and sometimes, exclusive access to online databases. As with the case of library "friend" organizations, your membership dollars go to preservation, special project, educational workshops and meetings, and additions to the organization's collections.

Genealogical and historical societies form a solid foundation upon which the genealogical community rests. But in many cases, this foundation is crumbling. Many societies are suffering from declining memberships and a crippling lack of volunteers. If these institutions that have given us so much are to survive, they need your support on both a local and national level. By helping societies, you are, in essence, helping yourself.

How to Choose
Like many of you, I suspect, I simply don't have the resources to join every society that I'd like to, so I have to pick and choose. But with so many worthwhile organizations, how do I decide?

The first thing I do is check out the organizations. What kind of publications do members receive? Will these publications help me with my research? What other research services are offered? Will I be able to take advantage of the organization's collections and resources—even if I don't live in the vicinity? Are there worthy projects in the works that I want to help support? Most societies now maintain a Web presence, and you may be able to find the answers to these questions and more online.

Links
Federation of Genealogical Societies
http://www.fgs.org

FGS Society Hall
http://www.familyhistory.com/societyhall/main.asp

National Genealogical Society
http://www.ngsgenealogy.org

Friends of Libraries, U.S.A.
http://www.folusa.com/

Beyond the Index

Tiogeeee or Not? Analyzing a Place of Birth
1 May 2002
Michael John Neill

M Y GRANDMOTHER'S DEATH CERTIFICATE, obituary, and marriage record all list her place of birth as Tioga, Hancock
County, Illinois. Two of these records are official documents and I
have copies of all these items for my files. Yet there is a problem
with these documents.

They all contain the "wrong" place of birth for my grandmother. While these records are "original" sources (and not a transcription or an abstract), they are not a primary source for my grandmother's date and place of birth. They were all created years after
her birth. The death certificate is a primary source but only for her
death and burial information, not her birth information. The marriage record is a primary source for her date and place of marriage,
but again not for her birth information. Both documents contain
information on my grandmother's place of birth. But because they
were recorded many years after my grandmother's birth, they are
not a primary source for her birth information. To top it off, my
own grandmother would not be considered a primary source for
information on her date and place of birth. In fact, none of us could

be a primary source for our own date and place of birth—we were all too young when it happened!

Just because a source is primary does not mean it is always correct. (On the other hand, just because a source is not primary does not mean it is incorrect.) A primary source for an event is a document that was created reasonably close to the time of the actual event from information obtained from someone who reasonably had first-hand knowledge of the event.

There are three documents that point to Grandma's date and place of birth. Two would be considered primary sources. The third source is circumstantial evidence that does not contradict the first two records. In some cases there will be no direct primary sources and a complete analysis of secondary sources is necessitated.

The first source is Grandma's birth record from 1910. Her birth certificate indicates she was born on 1 September 1910 in Elderville, Hancock County, Illinois. Elderville is a few miles east of Tioga, the town where Grandma thought she was born. The date of birth is the same one that Grandma always gave. The birth record, which could be wrong, is a primary source for information on my grandmother's date and place of birth.

The second source is Grandma's baptismal record from 1915. It was created five years after Grandma's birth, but it too indicates the exact same date and place of birth as the birth certificate. And Grandma, being five years old at the time is likely not the informant.

The third record is not a birth record. It just lends additional credence to Grandma's place of birth. In fact, Grandma is not even listed on this record. It is the 1910 census, taken the April before Grandma was born. Her parents are listed as living in Wythe Township, Hancock County, Illinois—the township that contains Elderville. This record is NOT proof that Grandma was born in Elderville. Grandma's father is listed as a farmer owning his own farm. While it is possible, the family likely did not move between the April date of the census and September when Grandma was born.

From Whence Tioga

Virtually every other record on my grandmother indicates her place of birth was Tioga, Hancock County, Illinois. This is because on almost every other record for my grandmother, my grandmother is the informant (or where the informant got their information). Grandma always thought she was born in Tioga (Grandma always pronounced the word "Tio gee"—rhymes with the golf term "bogey." Try finding that on a map!). Even after I discovered Grandma was not born where she thought she was, I rarely brought it up. It was not worth arguing about. I'm not certain exactly why Grandma thought she was born in Tioga, but it likely had to do with the fact that her father was born near there and that his family had lived in the area since the 1860s.

How Do I Handle This in My Own Records?

I record Grandma's place of birth in my records as Elderville, Hancock County, Illinois. However, I make a comment in my "notes" that Grandma believed she was born in Tioga (based upon conversations I had with her before she died). Consequently that village is listed as her place of birth on many of her records. It helps to explain the inconsistencies.

The Importance of Primary Sources!

Grandma's example brings home the importance of locating additional records and focusing on primary ones when they are available. In this case, some researchers might stop with a death and marriage record. After all, they provided consistent information regarding the place of birth. Why bother with the birth record when I already "have" the information it contains? This mindset can get us into trouble, especially in cases where the primary source is readily accessible and the person involved is a direct line ancestor. One may choose to not obtain birth certificates for third or fourth cousins. However, as a general rule I obtain records of vital events for all direct-line ancestors and even aunts and uncles where possible.

All Inconsistencies Go Away This Easily?

Of course not. Nor will you always be able to find as many records as are available in each case. What we can do, however, is transcribe each document exactly as it is written or extract the desired information verbatim. All of the varying locations or dates should at least be entered in our notes, although most programs will permit multiple dates of birth and death for an individual to be recorded. Personally, I prefer to make one "big" note for the specific event and include appropriate transcriptions relevant to the specific event instead of having a myriad of birth dates or places. In that note, I analyze the various information and state my conclusion. Including my reasoning is essential. This allows others to see my train of thought and decide whether they choose to agree with me or not. It also allows me to later read my reasoning and to decide for myself (perhaps in light of new information and knowledge) whether I wish to keep my original conclusion or change it.

"The farther backward you can look, the farther forward you are likely to see."

—*Sir Winston Churchill, 1874-1965*

More Born in Tiogeeee ... Follow-up
8 May 2002
Michael John Neill

LAST WEEK'S ARTICLE ON MY PATERNAL GRANDMOTHER'S place of birth generated a great deal of reader response. In brief, all primary data collected on Grandma's birth indicated she was born in Elderville, Wythe Township, Hancock County, Illinois. All records where Grandma was the informant indicated her birth in Tioga, Hancock County, Illinois.

The Metropolis of Elderville
There's not even a building in Elderville anymore. As several readers pointed out, Grandma really wasn't born in Elderville anyway. Grandma's birth was likely one of millions that took place on an outlying farm. Birth certificates for those born in rural areas are rarely specific enough to list an "exact" place of birth (such as "the birth took place in the southwest quarter of section five in Wythe Township"). Elderville likely was the town nearest to where the family lived in 1910 (the year of Grandma's birth) or possibly their post office address at that time. In some cases, the doctor might not have remembered where the birth took place and might have "guessed" as best he could.

Where Are These Places?

Elderville and Tioga, Illinois, can both be located on Mapquest <http://www.mapquest.com>. Readers who perform such a search will see that we are talking about a rural area of the state.

Maps of any region where family members lived are always helpful. In this case, there is an online map showing the townships in Hancock County, Illinois <http://www.outfitters.com/ illinois/hancock/twpmap_hancock.html.> Tioga (where Grandma said she was born) is in Walker township, directly south of Wythe Township (listed on the "official" records for Grandma's birth). Tioga is about a mile north of the Hancock County-Adams County line. Thankfully in this case there's no debate about the county of birth.

Topozone.com is another good place for locating places. Both villages can easily be located using the search interface at <http://www.topozone.com>.

Elderville
http://www.topozone.com/map.asp?z=15&n=4465603&e=644892&s= 50&loc=Elderville

Tioga
http://www.topozone.com/map.asp?z=15&n=4452287&e=640679&s= 50&loc=Tioga

At the 1:50,000 scale, the section numbers of the township are clearly shown in red. Readers who are familiar with the area or who took a look at the map may realize that there is not as much discrepancy between the two locations as one might think. Land and tax records for my grandmother's parents in 1910 should provide the exact location of their farm. This would not be proof of where Grandma was born, but if the farm is located in southern Wythe Township, it would even be closer to Tioga than the village of Elderville.

Did Grandma Mean She Was Born "in" Tioga?

When Grandma said she was born "in Tioga," I never thought she meant in the town itself. And I never asked her "just exactly how close to Tioga?" she meant. Even if I had asked such a question, it might not have been possible for her to be specific. Just how close to Tioga Grandma meant, I'm not certain. She might not have been either.

Did They Know Where They Were Living?

Obviously the family knew how to get to their home, but the names people sometimes use to refer to their residence may appear inconsistent. In some cases, they may refer to former names by which the location had been known. A certain area of a county, a township, or a city may be referred to by a former name or a nickname by some residents. As a result, this nickname for the location, perhaps known only to locals or "old-timers," may be used on various official records even though the place is no longer listed on any modern map.

Did They List a Nearby Large Town?

While not the case in Grandma's situation, some individuals may not give their actual place of birth. Instead, they may use the name of a nearby larger village or town, one more likely to be known by those not familiar with the area. I even do this myself. If someone from within ten or fifteen miles of where I live asks where I live, I'll give them the name of the town. If it's someone from within the state of Illinois, but outside our "local area" I'll tell them I live near Galesburg or a short distance from Moline, depending upon where I'm at. To others, I'll say two hours west of Chicago. It is easier than explaining the precise location to those not familiar with our local geography. I have several ancestors, especially those who were immigrants, who did the same thing on various records when listing their foreign place of birth or origin. Several listed their place of birth on some records not as the actual village in which they were born, but instead listed the county seat.

Grandma's Knowledge of Her Birth

Grandma is no longer living, so I can't ask her how she knew she was born in Tioga. Either her parents or another relative told her, or she just assumed it to be true. However she obtained the knowledge, she did not learn it from her own experience. If several different family members (old enough to reasonably have firsthand knowledge of the event) had told her the same thing, one could lend more credence to the Tioga place of birth. Of course, the secondary nature of Grandma's knowledge of her place of birth does not necessarily mean the place of birth she listed was incorrect. Indicating that a clue or piece of information is secondary does not mean the information is incorrect. It just means her knowledge of her place of birth was not first hand. If Grandma were alive, I could ask her how she knew she was born at Tioga. If I had asked her how she knew, she could thought that I was getting "uppity" or a "little big for my britches" and left the question unanswered. One sometimes has to watch how far one pushes one's questions.

It is worth remembering that if my knowledge of an event is secondary there is always the possibility that the primary source (either a document or a person) was intentionally incorrect. I don't think Grandma lied about her place of birth or that the person who told her lied to her. But I have seen cases where secondary sources were intentionally wrong, frequently to obscure the facts or make it impossible to find out the "real story."

Born at a Relative's House?

An expectant mother may stay with relatives in the later stages of her pregnancy and give birth to the child at that location instead of her actual residence. While this is a possibility in this case, I have no evidence (either on paper or from family lore) to support the "birth at a neighbor's" theory. The father had relatives who lived closer to Tioga, but the mother did not. In this case, the primary paper evidence (the birth record, the christening record, and the family's known 1910 residence) are all consistent with a birth in Wythe Township.

Some will fault me, but I'm going with the Wythe Township as Grandma's place of birth unless I locate some other record to the contrary. My reasoning basically boils down to the fact that all the "original" sources are consistent. If they were not consistent, the situation would be different. The Tioga information obtained from Grandma's marriage and death records will be clearly referenced in my notes. The upside to this situation is that all my work to "reconcile" the differences has lead me to more information on the family and their life around the time of Grandma's birth. And isn't that the goal of family history?

Is It a Big Deal in This Case?

Probably not. The names of Grandma's parents are not in question and the birth locations that I have are not all that different. In my case, Grandma's birth place is not a great genealogical mystery. Next week we'll look at my paternal grandmother's mother, born in 1874. This woman was born in Illinois, Iowa, or Missouri, depending upon which record one chooses to believe!

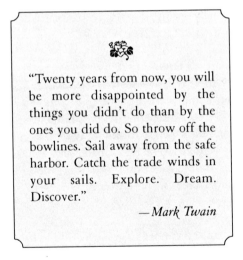

"Twenty years from now, you will be more disappointed by the things you didn't do than by the ones you did do. So throw off the bowlines. Sail away from the safe harbor. Catch the trade winds in your sails. Explore. Dream. Discover."

— *Mark Twain*

Born in the Tri-State Area—Literally
15 May 2002
Michael John Neill

PEOPLE TEND TO THINK I HAVE RESEARCHED all my dirt farming ancestors to the point where they are neat and clean and
that all my lines have been traced back to the beginning of time.
Nothing could be further from the truth.

Perhaps one of my biggest stumbling blocks centers on my
great-grandmother Ida May Sargent, born somewhere in 1874,
probably on 1 April. Information is relatively consistent in regards
to her date of birth. It is her place of birth that is the problem. The
problem is compounded by the fact that Ida was born at a time
when civil registrations of births were not kept in any of the three
states where she was possibly born.

Unfortunately I have no primary record for information on her
place of birth and must rely on secondary information for information on Ida's place of birth. Many research problems are aggra-
vated by such difficulties, especially as research progresses to earlier time periods. I would love to have a primary record of Ida's
birth, but I'm not holding my breath. The earliest record I have
that includes information in Ida's birth is her entry in the 1880 census, when she was approximately six years of age. This entry,

which lists her as Martha instead of Ida May, indicates she was born in Iowa.

How Do I Know It Is Her in the 1880 Census?

Since I wasn't there the day the 1880 census was taken, my conclusion has to be based on other records. However, I do feel fairly confident that I have the correct entry in the 1880 census for my great-grandmother. In this case, it is more than just a gut feeling. There are several pieces of information obtained from other sources that allowed me to comfortably conclude the six-year-old Martha listed in the 1880 census is actually my Ida.

- All information obtained on Ida, including official records and family sources, consistently indicate her parents were named Ira and Ellen Sargent.
- Ida is known to have a younger sister by a few years named Ella or Ellen.
- Court records for Ira Sargent in the early 1900s indicate he had a daughter Ida Trautvetter.
- Ida is known to have lived in Warsaw, Hancock County, Illinois, as a child.

And I remember that nicknames are persistent problems in census records. I also remember that our ancestors may occasionally be listed by nicknames they never actually used (Just like I am frequently listed by a nickname "Mike," which I have never used in my entire life—it's a fine name but I do not choose to use it). I also know that our ancestors were not always asked to "check" their entries in various records and that such name variants can easily happen.

As I tracked Ida through various other records, the places of birth were not as consistent as I had hoped. Her 1880 through 1920 census entries <http://www.rootdig.com/census/idasargent/> listed her as born in either Iowa or Missouri. The varying places of birth in the census, while frustrating, did not really concern or surprise me. Census records are frequently incorrect and one never knows who in the family actually gave the information to the census taker.

So Where Was Ida Born?
I really wish I knew.

Ida was born in many places, depending upon what record one chooses to believe:

- Alexandria, Clark County, Missouri—her son John's 1937 death certificate.
- Warsaw, Hancock County, Illinois—her obituary and family sources.
- Adams County, Illinois—her death certificate.
- Iowa—her 1898 marriage to George Trautvetter.
- Lima, Adams County, Illinois—her 1936 marriage to William Miller.

Obviously I have a problem here as a person can only be born in one physical location. Some analysis is therefore necessary. First, the towns are not as inconsistent as one might think. This is an excellent situation where a map of the region is helpful. All the specific towns are located within close proximity of each other. Warsaw, Illinois, and Alexandria, Missouri, are across the Mississippi River from each other. Lima, Illinois, is approximately fifteen miles from Warsaw. The state of Iowa is in very close proximity as well (a visit to <http://www.mapquest.com> will confirm the relative proximity of these locations).

Second, these variant locations cannot be easily dismissed through place name changes, misspellings, or county line or boundary changes (The Mississippi does change course, but Alexandria has stayed in Missouri and Warsaw has stayed in Illinois.) More work will have to be done to determine if there is an answer to this problem.

My Theory on the Locations
Since a person can only be born in one place, even if that place has had several names, my working theory is that these places likely had some significance to the family. Outright lies are possible as well. In this case, I use each new location as one more place to look for information, fully cognizant that only one is Ida's real place of

birth. Perhaps Ida lived in each of the places during her childhood. Perhaps one or both of Ida's parents lived in one of the places. Right now I just don't know.

What Was Going On in Their Minds

We do not know what went on in the mind of the informant when they were asked to provide information for a record. We also do not know exactly how the questioner posed the question either (did he really read it verbatim from the form?). Perhaps the informant interpreted the question as "where was your mother from" or "where was your mother's family from" instead of "where was your mother actually born?" The problem is that we cannot see or hear the actual interaction that took place between the person asking the question and the person providing the information. We only have the remaining document with the information it contains. And if the informant was not really certain of the answer, he might simply have guessed to shut the person up. After all, who would care in fifty years what the form said anyway?

In later columns, we'll follow my work on the origins of Ida. Unfortunately as I write this I do not already have the answer lying neatly in a file folder. If the answer is available, it is in some record I have yet to discover.

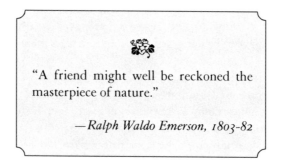

"A friend might well be reckoned the masterpiece of nature."

—*Ralph Waldo Emerson, 1803-82*

Starting with My Senses
22 May 2002
Michael John Neill

Note: This article is written under the assumption that the only information I have on Nazaire is what was obtained from his various census records. Copies of the family's census entire census entries are viewable at <http://www.rootdig.com/census/drollette/index.html>.

I RECENTLY WENT BACK TO AN OLD WORLDCONNECT <http://worldconnect.rootsweb.com> posting on one of my wife's families. The submission contained sketchy information on Nazaire/Isiah Drollette and his family in Saranac, Clinton County, New York. Before researching the family extensively in local records, and definitely before researching the family in Canada where Nazaire was born, I decided to locate Nazaire in as many census records as possible as I had ready access to these records through the images at Ancestry.com. The census entries would allow me to estimate a variety of dates and get an idea of the family structure. Once I had used them to establish a framework, searches would be conducted in other records to establish more firm connections, where possible.

The only information I had was that Nazaire was born in Canada ca. 1830, was married to Marie/Mary Maille (Maigge) in the late 1840s. He had several children, including one who likely was an ancestor of my wife. Nazaire was thought to have died sometime after 1900 and to have spent most of his time in the Saranac, New York area after his emigration from Canada. My census searches would start in Saranac. I was fortunate that Nazaire did not move much after his settlement in Saranac.

I began with the 1900 census and proceeded to work backwards, trying to follow the genealogical adage of working from the "present to the past." The censuses here have been abstracted for purposes of illustration. A census record should always be extracted completely. The other columns of information not included here can provide additional clues and may help in distinguishing one family from another.

The 1900 Census
1900 Census, Saranac, Clinton County, New York, enumeration district 30, sheet 11, page 221A, taken 15 June 1900 (abstracted entry)

Drollette, Isiah, Head: Apr 1827: Canada: Canada: Canada
—Eliza,Wife: June 1856: New York: Canada: Canada
—Lyman, Etta,dau: July 1882: New York: England: New York
—Drollette, Moses,son: Mar 1891: New York: New York: New York

Based upon the entry, Isiah and Eliza have been married twelve years. Eliza is the mother of one child, who is living. Children Etta and Moses are both listed as single. Eliza is not the name I had for Isiah's wife.

Even though I've seen no other census entries for this family, something seems awry with the entry. It appears (but is not explicitly stated) that either Eliza or Isiah has been married before. The census indicates they have been married for twelve years and child Etta is eighteen. It appears that Eliza was married before and Etta is her daughter by a previous marriage (Etta's father is listed as having been born in England). Moses' father should have been listed with a place of birth of Canada instead of New York. The number of children for Eliza does not coincide with this theory, but perhaps the question was interpreted as how many children were of this marriage. This census entry strongly indicates that other records should be searched.

The 1880 Census

1880 Census, Saranac, Clinton County, New York, enumeration district 34, dwelling 92, family 102, taken June 1880 [no date listed], (abstracted entry).

Isiah Draulette	self	50	Canada	Canada	Canada
Mary Draulette	wife	46	Canada	Canada	Canada
Elmore Draulette	son	24	New York	Canada	Canada
Josephine Draulette	daugh	17	New York	Canada	Canada
Napoleon Draulette	son	15	New York	Canada	Canada
Frank Draulette	son	12	New York	Canada	Canada
George Draulette	son	10	New York	Canada	Canada
Joseph Draulette	son	8	New York	Canada	Canada
Salina Draulette	daugh	3m	New York	Canada	Canada

It is really too bad there is no 1890 census entry for this family, twenty years is a long time. A lot can happen. Listed as aged fifty, Isiah would be born ca. 1830, according to this entry. This year of birth is reasonably consistent with the 1827 year of birth listed in the 1900 census. The name of the wife is now consistent with the name I had (which still does not mean it is correct). Mary (the wife in 1880) would have been born ca. 1834. This year of birth is twenty years earlier than the year of birth for wife Eliza listed in 1900. This wide discrepancy continues to hint at the more than one wife theory.

However, there are two possibilities. First, Isiah had two wives, Mary/Marie and Eliza. Or second, the Isiah I have in 1900 is not the same Isiah as I have in 1880. My research in the 1900 census should have included the ENTIRE Saranac district and not stopped with the first reasonable match. My research log should indicate whether or not I searched the entire district. If an entire search was not done, then I should go back and revisit the census. Until further work has been done on this family, it is always possible that there were two separate Isiahs. I should not let the unusual nature of the name lead me down the wrong path. Two additional comments here:

1. My grandfather with the most unusual name of John Ufkes had two first cousins with the same name. While it is an entirely different family in a completely different situation, it serves as a reminder that men or women can have the same unusual name.

2. I already think I know how many Isiahs there are, but am not saying for purposes of this illustration. And of course, I could always be wrong myself!

Our analysis of the census entries for Nazaire is only partially complete. Next week we'll visit him in the 1850-70 census entries and discuss some possible ways to continue the research beyond the census.

"To me every hour of the day and night is an unspeakably perfect miracle."

—*Walt Whitman, 1819-92*

Starting with My Senses, Part 2
29 May 2002
Michael John Neill

THIS WEEK WE CONTINUE OUR ANALYSIS of the census entries for the family of Nazaire/Isiah Drollette in upstate New York (Part 1 is at <http://www.ancestry.com/rd/prodredir.asp?sourceid=831&key=A577401>.) Our census work is not done until we have located all the entries for this individual and his family. Copies of the family's entire census entries are viewable at <http://www.rootdig.com/census/drollette/index.html>.

The 1870 Census
Saranac, Clinton County, New York, family and dwelling number 18, pages 3-4, taken 2 August 1870 (abstracted entry).

Drulette, Isiah	40	M	Canada
Drulette, Sarah	35	F	Canada
Drulette, Julia	19	F	New York
Drulette, Isiah	18	M	New York
Drulette, Mary	16	F	New York
Drulette, Elmore	14	M	New York
Drulette, Salinda	12	F	New York

Drulette, Louisa	10	F	New York
Drulette, Josephine,	6	F	New York
Drulette, Napolean,	5	M	New York
Drulette, John,	3	M	New York
Drulette, George,	8/12	M	New York (born in October)

The wife has a different name than the one listed in the 1870 census, but based upon the names of the children, I've located the correct family. Many of the younger children from 1870 are listed in 1880. The older ones not listed are probably on their own now, and it is possible that some died between the 1870 and 1880 census. There is also the possibility that some are listed under different names. The twelve-year-old Frank in 1880 might be the three-year-old John in 1870. A middle name might have been used or the child might have had a christening name and a different name as he got older. Further work will have to be done on the children to determine exactly how many there really are. Censuses alone will not provide all the answers.

Is Sarah of 1870 the Mary of 1880? Based solely upon this record I'm not certain. However, the years of birth for the Sarah of 1870 (ca. 1835) and the Mary of 1880 (ca. 1834) are not significantly different. The ages are consistent enough to be the same person and to be different from the Eliza listed as the wife in 1900. More work still needs to be done.

The 1860 Census

Saranac, Clinton County, New York, dwelling 1125, family 1062, page 167, taken 5 October 1860 (abstracted entry).

Isiah Draulet	30	M	Canada
Mary	28	F	Canada
Julia	10	F	New York
Isiah	9	M	New York
Mary	6	F	New York
Elmon	5	M	New York
Lucinda	3	F	New York
Louisa	1	F	New York

The family names, with the exception of Lucinda, are fairly close to the names in the other census entries. The wife's name is now back to Mary and the wife (if it is the same one) only aged seven years from 1860 to 1870, something not unheard of with census records. The age difference alone would not be enough to assume a different wife. With the exception of the 1900 census, Isiah's ages have been unusually consistent from the 1860 through the 1880 censuses.

The 1850 Census
Saranac, Clinton County, New York, dwelling 192, family 196, taken 7 December 1850 (abstracted entry).

Nazer Draulette	22	M	Canada
Mary Draulette	18	F	Canada
Married within the census year			

This is the earliest entry for Nazaire, who is listed under the spelling Nazer. There were no other entries for surnames reasonably close to our focus person in the 1850 census. The ages of this couple are consistent with the ages of the couple in 1860. The fact that the couple was married within the census year for the 1850 census is consistent with the age of their oldest child in 1860. The statement "within the census year" for the 1850 census means a range of dates between 1 June 1849 and 31 May 1850. This gives us an approximate date of marriage for the couple.

Getting the Children's Ages
For now, if the names are different, I'm going to consider them different children. Based upon additional research or analysis, I may "merge" children, but charting them all may help me to line things out. Some of the children listed in the various census records follow:

Name	1860	1870	1880	Born?
Julia	Aged 10	Aged 19	---	Ca. 1850-1851
Isiah	Aged 9	Aged 18	---	Ca. 1851-1852
Mary	Aged 6	Aged 16	---	Ca. 1854

39

| Louisa | --- | Aged 1 | Aged 10 | Ca. 1859-1860 |
| Napolean | --- | Aged 5 | Aged 15 | Ca. 1865 |

Personally, I always consider a census age suspect and insert "ca." in front of any year of birth obtained from a census record.

Summary

1. Analyze as many census entries as you can for the family under study.

2. Copy the entire census entry—not just the summary you see here that provided the fodder for our discussion.

3. Copy the census information verbatim—do not attempt to correct or make alterations a century and a half after the fact.

4. Just because two records are consistent does not necessarily mean that they are correct—it just means they are consistent.

Follow-up

Now that I have completed the census work for Nazaire, I will begin searching for him and his family in other records in Clinton County, New York. Given that the family was French-Canadian, records from local Catholic churches may be the best place to start. Based upon the five census entries, I have a good idea of the family structure (or at least the children of Nazaire). The censuses did not provide me with exact dates of birth, but they did allow me to approximate the birth year for each child and for the parents. Months of birth were given for Nazaire, his 1900 wife Eliza, and his child George. These should be double-checked against other records where possible. My search for Nazaire's Canadian origins is best put on hold until I know more about him in New York State.

What Should I Do?

1. Visit the USGenWeb page for Clinton County, New York, via <http://www.usgenweb.org>.

2. Consider posting a query for this family on the boards at Ancestry.com at <http://boards.ancestry.com>. (For more on message board posting, read "Before You Post" at <http://www.ancestry.com/library/view/news/articles/5178.asp> and "After You Post" at <http://www.ancestry.com/library/view/news/articles/5254.asp>.)

3. Learn about records in New York State using the Research Guide from the Family History Library <http://www.familysearch.org/Eng/Search/RG/frameset_rhelps.asp>. (Click on "N" for New York.)

4. Search the Family History Library Card Catalog at <http://www.familysearch.org> for items on Clinton County, New York, in their collection

New York has a wonderful series of state census records that would also be helpful in researching this family. A future follow-up in this series will discuss applicable state census records for this family. Ancestry's *The Source* has information on state census records. Many state archives have state census records in their collection as does the Family History Library. Those wishing to locate information on state census records may wish to type (without the quotes):

"[your state] state census records"

into a search engine such as Google <http://www.google.com> to locate more information. Readers who are really lucky may find transcriptions of such records online; more likely one will find bibliographies and finding aids.

References

Szucs, Loretto and Sandra H. Luebking. *The Source: A Guidebook of American Genealogy, revised* (Salt Lake City, Utah: Ancestry, 1997.)
http://www.ancestry.com/rd/prodredir.asp?sourceid=831&key=P1026

Along Those Lines

Stop Procrastinating! Organize Your Family Reunion in 2002!
3 May 2002
George G. Morgan

A GENTLEMAN AT A GENEALOGY SEMINAR recently told me that he has wanted to organize a family reunion for a long time. He said he had read my book *Your Family Reunion: How to Plan It, Organize It, and Enjoy It*, and though he felt the information was well-written and easy to follow, he was afraid he had waited too late to start working on a reunion for 2002. What worried him the most was that there are a number of older relatives he wanted everyone in the family to have the opportunity to get to know before it was too late. He knew he had procrastinated long enough, but he wanted my opinion on whether it was too late to plan a family reunion for this year.

The answer to the question is an emphatic, "It is never too late to plan a family reunion of some sort." In "Along Those Lines . . ." this week, I want to help you understand how you really can still get a family reunion off the ground for 2002.

What Qualifies as a Reunion?

Whether you realize it or not, you have probably organized any number of family reunions in the past. The most typical family reunion occurs over the dinner table. You experience a type of family reunion every day when you and your family gather for a meal, to watch television, to go to a movie together, or just go for a walk.

Anytime a group of family members gets together to share time and information, that qualifies a reunion. However, the term "family reunion" usually evokes a mental image of a huge group of family members in some sort of a formally organized event, maybe even at a hotel, restaurant, or other fancy venue. That does not need to be the case. Every family gathering, regardless of size, will involve some planning, communication, and organization. Smaller reunions require some of this work, and larger reunions typically require even more of this preparation. And the more "frills" you add, the more involved the planning and organization becomes.

What is most important is that family members have the opportunity to build relationships and share information. Any family reunion is an opportunity to share those interesting family stories and traditions, and to get people interested in their family heritage. You get the people together and supply the opportunity to communicate, and a great deal will happen all by itself.

Who Says Size Isn't Important?

The size and scope of your family reunion are the most important factors determining whether you can or cannot quickly organize the event this year. The size and scope will be determined by a number of factors. These include the size of the family, their ages, where they live, how far they will have to travel, the type of reunion, any special activities you might plan to offer, and the expense involved. You certainly want to make sure that everyone who wants to attend the reunion can do so. You also want it to be within the financial means of every participant.

A small reunion can be an intimate affair, ranging in size from just a few people to perhaps twenty or twenty-five family members. An event this size can usually be organized and managed quite simply by one to three people and can typically be organized within a short period of time. It can be complicated when out-of-town relatives are invited, but that may be simplified by having some or all of them stay in people's homes. There is also the advantage that meals and other events may be held in someone's home, in a small rented hall, or as a barbeque in a park.

The amount of planning, organization, and logistical work expands as the size of a group increases. A medium-size reunion might consist of between twenty-five and fifty attendees. Depending on the age mix of the group, planning can become more complicated as well. Seldom can a group this size be accommodated at someone's home, and so it becomes imperative to locate a venue for the event. Sleeping accommodations, transportation to/from the airport and special events, meals and other entertainment can add to the complexity of the planning and to the on-site management of the event. As you plan more activities, the cost may increase as well. It will be very important to get a grasp of the finances early on so that attendees can be charged an appropriate fee to cover all the expenses.

A large family reunion may present some interesting challenges, but they also are full of rewards. When working with a larger group, one of fifty or more people, the amount of advance planning and the lead times required increases dramatically. It may be more difficult to locate and schedule hotels and other facilities to accommodate a group that size unless you work far in advance of the dates. Meals, banquets, entertainment, special events, transportation, and other considerations will also need careful attention to ensure their success. When the size of your group exceeds one hundred people, you may even want to consider hiring a professional party planner whose experience and expertise can help guarantee greater success.

Are you overwhelmed? Well don't be! The medium-size and large reunion also can be designed to be a less formal, less expensive, and overall highly enjoyable affair—and can be organized on shorter notice than you might think.

Heading Down the Fast Path

When I wrote my book, it was my intention to provide as complete a description to the process and as many tips and suggestions as possible. I have done a substantial amount of professional corporate meeting and conference planning in my life, and I plan seminars and workshops all the time. Family reunion planning, therefore, came naturally to me as a result of this professional work. My book will provide a structured process for anyone doing family reunion planning, from the largest gala event all the way down to the smallest backyard family gathering. What is important, though, is thinking through all the details.

Let me provide you with an excellent personal example. One side of my MORGAN family in North Carolina holds a family reunion each fall for an average of one hundred people, sometimes more. The family has simplified the process each year so that now it is almost rote.

The date is communicated three to six months in advance and the location is always the same. The communication process isn't complicated. Family members split the list of relatives into groups of five to six families and either make telephone calls or send e-mail. They ask for a confirmation back via telephone or e-mail by a certain date, but this is a very flexible thing, too. After the confirmation date, the "callers" then coordinate back with one another so that we know who will and will not be able to attend.

The reunion is always held on a Saturday afternoon in the park-like setting of my Cousin Rita's side yard at the old family farm. Under a canopy of huge trees, beside her rustic flower garden and overlooking a pond, the family holds a covered-dish meal. Relatives travel there from as far away as Pennsylvania and Florida, and stay with other relatives in the area. Every family brings something in the way of food or supplies, and everyone bring their own lawn chairs. Some people even bring folding tables to contribute to the outdoor setup. There is always a wonderful camaraderie and an overabundance of food. As one of the two family genealogists, I always bring charts and forms with me, and we encourage family members to bring old photographs, Bibles, and other items to show and share stories. (And you'd better believe I am prospecting this family gold mine!)

In this scenario, please note that the organization is amazingly simple. Most important, the amount of lead time, communication expense, and individuals' cost are minimal. A few people communicate to family members, one person provides her yard as the venue, everyone contributes a food dish or supplies, everyone helps with setting up and cleanup, and a great time is had by all. When we talk about this reunion, we realize that since everyone already knows it will take place in September or October, the lead time for communicating and organizing could probably be done with little more than a month's notice.

Planning for Success
If you are organizing your first family reunion, the lead time may need to be greater because of the advance communications required. If you are planning to hire a facility or congregate at a hotel, there will be other factors to consider and plan. Your goal is to host a pleasant, memorable reunion, and perhaps it will become an annual event. The event will require planning and some on-site organization to insure success, but there is no reason this should require a full year.

There is still time to organize a successful family reunion for 2002. It's time to stop procrastinating and time to start doing some planning. It's not too late!

Happy Family Reunion Planning!

George

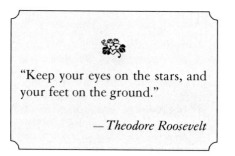

"Keep your eyes on the stars, and your feet on the ground."

— *Theodore Roosevelt*

Using a Handheld for Genealogy
10 May 2002
George G. Morgan

THE TECHNOLOGICAL INNOVATIONS WE HAVE SEEN SINCE the introduction of the personal computer twenty years ago have been nothing less than astounding. My first computer was purchased, used, from a colleague at work in 1985—an IBM PC with a whopping 4 MB of RAM and a 40 MB hard disk. "I'll never fill that up," I declared naively.

Nine months later, I ordered a new computer from Zeos with a 286 processor, 8 MB of RAM, and a 120 MB hard disk. "Now I'm set," I thought, again naively. It wasn't long until I had to increase the RAM to 16 MB just so I could migrate up to Windows 95.

I have since learned not to try to anticipate what I'll be needing tomorrow. My latest desktop computer has an AMD Athlon processor, 512 MB of RAM, a 5 GB hard disk, a ZIP disk, a CD-ROM drive, and a CD burner. We won't even talk about all the peripherals—except for the newest little addition, a handheld device. Often referred to as a PDA, or Personal Digital Assistant, these little devices have come of age and can be a real boon to helping organize your life. In addition, they now can help you with your genealogy research.

In "Along Those Lines . . ." this week, let's explore a little of the magic of the PDA, which is something I've been doing since I got one for Christmas.

What Is a PDA?

Personal Digital Assistants (PDAs) are not new. They have been around for years in various forms. I guess the first portable calculators might be loosely considered a form of PDA because they were your first personal, portable computer. However, the first real PDA was Apple Computer's Newton. It wasn't long before other portable, handheld computer devices were introduced. Some early ones boasted a 25,000-word dictionary and/or thesaurus, with perhaps a built-in calculator. Next came ones into which you could enter telephone numbers and addresses.

Over time, with the further miniaturization of component parts and the increasing amounts of storage, the capabilities of PDAs have expanded. So have the choices, both in hardware, in storage amounts, and in the numbers and types of programs available for the PDA users. The prices vary all over the place, from under $100 to well over $400, and models are available with both black-and-white or color display screens (with significant price differentials). You can spend still more money on software accessories.

Today's PDAs are still small, perhaps the size of a calculator. Just like the home computer, there are several operating systems available, depending on the make of PDA you choose. It appears that the Palm OS is the operating system being used in the most models of PDAs. This is important because it means that there appear to be more programs being developed for this operating software. The Palm brand, Handspring, and Sony PDAs all use the Palm OS. Check with the sales person regarding other brands and the operating system used by those brands. I'm not saying those are any less impressive PDAs, but your choice of a PDA and its operating system will definitely influence what you can obtain to run on your PDA.

What Can a PDA Do?

I received a Sony Clie for Christmas. Mine is the model PEG-T415, which has a black-and-white display screen. It comes with a cradle, into which I set the PDA in order to recharge it and to synchronize data with my desktop computer (more on that later). The software that came with the Clie was impressive. It has an address book for names, addresses, telephone numbers, e-mail addresses, and all other types of data. The Calendar scheduling software allows for the entry of dates and appointments, and you can set it up to set off a reminder alarm. (There are also three different types of travel alarms built into the unit too.) The TO-DO list and the Memo are simple to use and provide a quick place to jot notes. Ah! Jotting notes! Yes, you can do this easily enough with a program called Graffiti. Using the PDA's stylus, you can input letters, numbers, symbols, and punctuation on the screen. Graffiti is so very simple! There is a calculator, of course. There's also a program called World Mate to keep track of time around the world, which can convert currency, clothing sizes, and measurements, and contains the telephone code for many countries all over the globe. This little unit also comes with a sound program, a graphic viewer to view .JPG files, and other programs. The Clie interfaces with Microsoft Word and Excel to allow you to place documents created on your desktop computer on the PDA and vice versa. Very slick!

There also are other programs that can be installed to handle e-mail, access the Internet, get materials from news services and stock quote services, and more. These require the installation of the software, and the addition of a separately purchased wireless modem. You also need to set up a wireless communications account with a provider though I haven't connected this to my PDA yet. You can even explore GPS satellite software!

My Clie PDA's cradle is plugged into an electrical outlet and attaches to the desktop computer using a USB connection cable to allow the movement of data. (Some PDAs use the older, traditional serial cable connection, but USB is becoming more prevalent in all new computers.) I can enter data into the Clie; software on the desktop or into the PDA. I can then place the PDA in the cradle, where it is recharged, and/or initiate a Hot Sync so that the data on each computing device is synchronized and made the same. Also, when you have something new to install on the PDA, such as new software or copies of Word or Excel documents, you simply add them to a list on the desktop computer's Clie desktop, and they will be transferred/installed the next time you perform a Hot Sync. The Hot Sync is as simple as pressing a button on the front of the PDA.

How Can a PDA Help with My Genealogy?

At last we come to the crux of this column. I knew in advance that the PDA could allow me to make notes and do other tasks while I am traveling. However, I was unprepared for the existence of genealogy software for the PDA. Other titles, including language translation dictionaries, may prove useful to you, too.

While I was allowing the PDA to charge for the first time, I eagerly visited the PalmGear.com site at <http://www.palm gear.com> to see what accessories and software might be available. There are hundreds of software titles available and fifteen titles listed when I searched "genealogy" in the software area. Four programs are listed that allow you to take your genealogy data with you on your Palm OS PDA: MyRoots, HandyTree, GedStar, and GenWise.

There are also several programs that allow you to create a TO-DO list of research you need or want to note. The GenRes and GenResHDB database let you keep track of what resources you have used so as to prevent duplicate research. Cemetery lets you keep track of your cemetery research, including names, cemetery location, location of the plot, type of disposition (burial, entombment, cremation), and other data. Calendar Conversions is software that converts between Julian, Gregorian, Jewish, French Republic calendars, and the Julian day number. And Genealogy 1.0 allows you to use your wireless connection to look up your ancestor on the Internet.

I decided to try one of the programs for myself: MyRoots 1.70. I ordered it online for $17. To obtain and install it, you first download the trial version at the PalmGear.com site, unzip the compressed files, and install two of them on your PDA. Next, I received an e-mail from the software developer, Tapperware, as confirmation of my order. That e-mail provided me with a registration number. I had to open the MyRoots software on the PDA and enter the number, and this activated the software for full use. (I goofed on my first attempt at this, but the e-mail customer support people were wonderfully helpful.) Next, I downloaded the free MyRoots Conversion Utility 1.70 from the PalmGear.com site. What this does is convert a GEDCOM file you produce to a format usable by the PDA and by MyRoots.

My next step was to open my regular genealogy program, and create a new GEDCOM file. (Since I'm not sharing this data at this point, I didn't privatize the file for living individuals.) Next, I ran the MyRoots Conversion Utility to produce the new file. This file was automatically placed in the Clie queue for the next Hot Sync. Next, I placed the Clie in the cradle and ran the Hot Sync, and the data was downloaded to the PDA. I opened MyRoots and was prompted that there was a new file to be imported. I verified that I wanted to import the file and it started running. In a matter of ten minutes, I now had my full database on the PDA and could take it with me to the library. I can also enter new data into the MyRoots database as I go, using the Graffiti software.

MyRoots also comes with a user guide explaining the intricacies of uploading, merging, or synchronizing data between the PDA and the genealogy database on the desktop computer. It isn't as simple as it might be, but it can certainly be done.

Now, if I installed one of the PDA research resource software packages, I could have, essentially, a PDA-based research log. With the addition of a wireless modem and a provider, I could send e-mail to others with whom I am collaborating and I could connect to the Web for online research there, too.

The Possibilities

As I said, I am just getting started with this research tool. As time goes by, I plan to install other PDA software listed above and will be looking in *Genealogical Computing* and other locations for new information about using my PDA in my genealogical research. In the meantime, I am excited about this new "toy" and am looking forward to having it as a companion on many upcoming research trips.

Happy Hunting!

George

Writing History from Photographs
17 May 2002
George G. Morgan

I'VE BEEN SPENDING TIME RECENTLY looking through our family photographs. These range from the more recent ones to the oldest ones I have, which date from the early 1870s. I consider myself fortunate to have this rich visual legacy of my family and, although there are chronological gaps and missing images of some family members, these provide a vivid representation of the family's appearance over time.

Over the years, I have written a number of detailed biographical sketches of certain ancestors. Some years ago I wrote mini-histories of my great-grandfathers for a Floyd County, Georgia, book to honor them. Recently, however, I have begun considering a broader work about each of these two branches of the family and have been reviewing the family pictures looking for inspiration.

It is possible to write a compelling biography or family history using photographs. I've done this before and want to share a few thoughts about the technique in "Along Those Lines . . ." this week.

A Good Place to Start
We've been told by genealogists many, many times to start with ourselves and work backwards. I think our approach to reviewing

photographs and biographical material tends to be in chronological sequence. After all, that's how we live our lives. What I have done with the photographs I have of the people about whom I plan to write is compile them in chronological sequence. I place them in archival safe photographic accordion file folders by family.

The most important job is to properly identify the subjects in the photos and the locations. This is emphatically not the easiest part of the process. If you're lucky, someone in the family has already done much of this work and labeled the photos. If not, you will need to make this a high priority. You may want to consider making complete sets of photocopies and sending them off to relatives and old family friends to help with the identification process. On the photocopies, you can always make notations of those who have been identified and/or circle people with whom you need help.

The study of the type of photograph, the card stock on which it is mounted, the card stock's color, embossing, and edge treatment all help you home in on a time period.

Clothing can be a tremendous help in identifying people in the photographs. It takes a little study but you can learn about clothing fashion for men, women, and children and use this knowledge to isolate the subjects to a specific time frame. For instance, on one style of women's dress I found in a photograph, I noted the balloon shoulders and could therefore say that the photograph was taken after a specific date. In another, the striped stockings and dress worn by a baby boy helped determine the time period for that photograph.

Another approach to the identification process is to review the photos you have and to (A) use family resemblance to help group people together, and/or (B) use a process of elimination to home in on who a person is NOT and then speculate on who the person IS. Sometimes for me it has been a combination of the two. In one group of photos taken by my grandparents and great-aunts and -uncles in the early 1900s, I employed an interesting and rewarding process. The subjects included my grandmother and grandfather, before their marriage in 1908. Four of my grandmother's five sisters were included, as well as another man. I needed to isolate who was who. With the four sisters, it took some careful examination of the photos with a magnifying glass to verify the identities of three of them. Their identities were confirmed by using other, later picture. The fourth woman was a problem. It was not until I sent copies to a cousin who had different photos taken at the same time that I was able to make the necessary connection. My cousin copied her photos for me. The plaid, full-length skirt enabled me to verify that it was the same person, and, with the aid of my magnifying glass, I was able to connect the sister to an previously identified professionally taken photograph from a few years later. Success!

Next, I work my way through the collection, not once but twice. First I work through the file in chronological sequence, and then I work backward. I make sure that I have the photos in the right order. This means trying to group them into what might have been the right order both by year and then by season of the year.

Next I try to determine just where the photograph was taken. Photographers' imprints on card mountings can be helpful. If you find multiple pictures taken some time apart by the same photography studio, this could indicate that the subject lived close by. If you find a single photograph like this, it could be a secondary source of verification of residence. Look, too, at casual photographs for clues to location: landmarks, street signs, business names, events— all of these can contribute to identification of place, and sometimes the date.

Writing the Story
The old adage "A picture is worth a thousand words" really is true. For a writer, a photographic image of an ancestor in a certain locale at a specific point in time can translate into a rich narrative. For example, I wrote:

"On 28 May 1900, Green Berry Holder filed an application with the United Daughters of the Confederacy to be considered for the award of a Confederate Cross of Honor. At that time, he was living in Lindale, Georgia. It was not until 1912 that the honor was bestowed.

"On the appointed day, Green Berry arrived at the Civic Auditorium in downtown Rome, Georgia, with his wife, Penelope, for the awards ceremony. At sixty-seven, he still cut quite a figure. He was five feet ten inches tall and slender, sporting a full grey moustache and beard down

to the middle of his chest—so full and brushed so that his mouth was not visible. He was dressed in a frockcoat and vest, a black round-top hat with a silk band, his cravat completely hidden by his beard. His gold watch chain stretched across his torso and the timepiece rested in a vest pocket."

A further description of the ceremony, the speakers and the presenter from a newspaper account of the event, as well as a description of the venue as shown in a photograph in the newspaper, would contribute to the text concerning Green Berry. Additional descriptive material about Mrs. Holder also would be appropriate to incorporate her into the event. And while no mention was made of other family members' attendance, you can be sure that some or all of the local family were there. Perhaps additional material about other Confederate veterans on whom the UDC bestowed the Confederate Cross of Honor would be appropriate, especially if the rest of the biography described interaction with some of these old friends and colleagues.

The use of "props" such as buildings, automobiles, pets, furniture, tools, and other things you see in the pictures, can add atmosphere. They bring the stories to life and help humanize the subject.

Incorporating Other Facts

The research you have compiled over the years should provide you with a rich set of details. For instance, I could include the information from the marriage certificate, including the names of the clergy and witnesses. Information on where the person lived and with whom can be derived from census records, along with the occupation and the value of the property. I could even provide a description of the death, funeral, and interment from the obituary. A visit to the cemetery and photographs of gravestones, dates, and epitaphs add to the story.

Pulitzer Prize?

My motivation is not to win a literary award for my work, although I do want to produce a quality piece of work. My goal, and probably yours too, is to document the collected facts into some semblance of factual (not fictional) biography to preserve the story of the ancestors. I'll never win a Pulitzer Prize. My reward will be compiling quality family historical information. Not only will the photographs contribute to the text, they can complement it when I publish the history.

Research, methodology, planning, and dedication to documenting the facts (complete with citation of your sources): these are the components of writing a quality history. But organize and date those old photographs, identify the people and the places that are portrayed, and let the photographs speak to you. You'll find that the stories may write themselves because your ancestors will come back to life in front of your eyes.

Happy Writing!

George

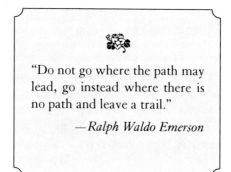

"Do not go where the path may lead, go instead where there is no path and leave a trail."

—*Ralph Waldo Emerson*

Attending a Conference in Absentia
24 May 2002
George G. Morgan

DRAT! I MISSED ANOTHER ONE. Last week, the National Genealogical Society held its annual conference in Milwaukee, Wisconsin, and I wasn't able to attend. Like many other people, I had other commitments and that, combined with the expenses associated with traveling and attending the conference, I just couldn't make the trip. That doesn't mean that I didn't just fidget all week long just imagining what I was missing. But while I could not attend this particular conference, it certainly doesn't mean I have to miss out on absolutely everything. And that is the focus of "Along Those Lines . . ." this week: how to participate in a large genealogy conference in absentia.

The Joys of Attending a Conference
Longtime readers of this column know how much emphasis I place on continuing your lifelong learning experience in any area of your personal interest. Genealogy and family history research are certainly no exception, especially when you consider the incredible array of materials that can be used to gather genealogically significant data, coupled with the range of record repositories where the records are to be located. Almost every record type and/or repository has something

unique about it, and we all need continuing education in order to fully use and take advantage of the information that can be gleaned from them.

Continuing to read about genealogy is one solid way to continue your education, but attending a genealogy conference is the epitome of the learning experience on many levels indeed. Regardless of the size and location of the conference, there is always something special to be learned. This applies to the local meeting of your own local genealogical society, a one- to two-hour genealogy workshop presented at your local public library, a state conference, or a regional or national conference presented by one of the national societies or an institution. There even are a few international conferences. And part of your lifelong learning involves looking for announcements of upcoming conferences, even one to several years in advance, so that you can plan and budget to attend.

I love attending genealogical conferences on many levels. First and foremost is the thrill of discovery. Everywhere I go at a conference, there are opportunities to discover more and more. One opportunity certainly involves attending the scheduled workshop sessions. People with knowledge, expertise, and real-world research examples can bring a focus to areas with which I may or may not have had personal experience. And I don't limit myself to "just" those research areas concentrated on MY genealogy; I attend other sessions on other research types to gain new perspectives and new ideas about research approaches. For example, attending a session about researching African American slave ancestors before the Civil War has provided me with clues to how to research my own female and/or less-than-affluent ancestors. Why? Because female ancestors, poor or migrant farming ancestors, and African American slaves were not enumerated by name prior to the 1850 U.S. Federal censuses, and the scarcity of records can present huge research brick walls. Not only did the session present a fascinating new historical view to me to incorporate into my own understanding of the times in which my ancestors lived, but I got new ideas for researching my unremarkable ancestors—and I subsequently made progress on some whose lives had been dead ends for years.

Workshops are far from the only opportunities to learn. Every other attendee has a story to tell—and probably multiple ones. I cringe to think that people who meet me at conferences make the assumption, "Well, George wouldn't be interested in what I have to say. He's a writer and knows all that stuff. He'd be bored to tears and doesn't want to deal with what I have to say." Nothing could be further from the truth! I've been working on my own family research for many years, but it is precisely this sharing of stories that helps me learn more. I don't have French or Italian or Scandinavian ancestors, but learning about the histories of these areas and the records produced there helps puts my own European ancestral research into a broader perspective. Best of all, striking up casual conversations can form new relationships of all types. I love meeting people and hearing the stories, and love to share my own, too. (Yes, you'll have to bear with listening to my stories, too!) We learn from one another outside of the formal workshops. That's why informal discussions before and after workshops, in the hallways, in the vendor area, over meals, and in the local libraries and archives is so very important—and fun.

And don't forget the vendor area. Get ready for major book lust when you see all the books, journals, CD-ROMs, tools, products, clothing, and other offerings you'll see at a conference. It's like being in a genealogy candy store. Browsing and spot reading can help you learn, too. The vendor representatives, however, are often goldmines of information. The booksellers have to be experts in order to prosper. They need to know which books to purchase for their inventories, and they are often willing to discuss what things they didn't bring to the conference and to point you to other books and resources which might complement or supplement what they sell.

But What if You Couldn't Go to the Ball?
Are you drooling yet? Well, I certainly am. I always regret not being able to attend every single conference, especially the national ones. The two biggies in the U.S. are presented annually by the National Genealogical Society (NGS) and by the Federation of Genealogical Societies (FGS) and are held in a different location each year.

The NGS Conference is held in the spring, and it was that conference that I had to miss last week in Milwaukee. Their conference next year will be held in Pittsburgh, Pennsylvania, on 28-31 May 2003. The FGS Conference is held in the second half of the year. This year's conference will be held in Ontario, California, on 7-10 August 2002. Next year's conference will be held on 3-6 September 2003 in Orlando, Florida. (Yes, Disney World, Universal Studios, SeaWorld's Shamu, AND genealogy all in the same place!) What this means is that you can still make plans and budget for coming conferences.

However, if you have to miss a conference, you can still capture some of the content from the workshop sessions. How? Through purchasing the conference syllabus and/or an audiotape recording. What a concept!

The conference syllabi produced by both NGS and FGS are large volumes containing the speakers' handout materials of almost all the presentations. Speakers submit their handouts and they are compiled, indexed, and printed. Every paid attendee receives a copy, but both NGS and FGS print additional copies for subsequent sale to people like us who miss the conferences. You can purchase a single year's conference syllabus or, in some cases, get a package deal on multiple years' syllabi. These publications are available at the NGS website's publications webpage <http://www.ngsgenealogy. org> and at the FGS Online Store webpage <http://fgs.org/fgs-onlinestore.htm>. I have built a personal reference library of conference syllabi because they often provide terrific "how-to" advice concerning all types of research.

While the printed syllabi are invaluable reference resources, reading a handout is only an outline of the material presented in each session. Both NGS and FGS make arrangements for workshop sessions to be recorded to audiotape if the speaker grants permission. The tapes are professionally taped and cassettes are sold, both at the conference and subsequently. Tape sales are brisk at the conference, purchased by people who had to choose between TWO concurrent sessions they wanted to attend, and by those who want to hear the session again. For people like me, I purchase a copy of the syllabus, review the topics and the handouts, and then order the audiotapes I want after the conference. A professional conference taping company named

Repeat Performance has been the vendor performing the taping for both NGS and FGS for a number of years, and you can order all the available tapes from past genealogy conferences at <http://www.audiotapes.com>. Later, I can listen to the tapes again and again, and can follow along with the syllabus. Question and answer periods are also included on many of the tapes.

Is It a Viable Substitute?

There really is nothing like attending a conference in person. Once you have been to an NGS and FGS conference, you'll be hooked. There literally is something for everyone, and you will find hundreds of other people who share this insane interest in family history research all in one place. Are the printed syllabi and the audiotapes a viable substitute for being there? They certainly provide one method for you to participate in absentia in a conference. While there is nothing like being there, they provide invaluable tools for you to continue your lifelong learning in genealogy. And your lifelong learning is, after all, part of what I call "the thrill of the chase" in family history research.

Visit the websites for NGS and FGS and check their online stores for syllabus availability, and then visit the site to check the availability of tapes. Once you experience a taped workshop, you'll recognize the value of this way of attending a conference in absentia. And then you'll really want to be there for the next one.

And remember, the next one is sponsored by FGS in Ontario, California, in less than three months. They're still accepting reservations. "Conference for how many?"

Happy conferencing in absentia!

George

Avoiding the Theft of Your Identity
31 May 2002
George G. Morgan

THE RECENT JOINT RESOLUTION AND PETITION from the Federation of Genealogical Societies and the National Genealogical Society states that, "According to the First Amendment Coalition, recent studies confirm that most identity thefts occur through the literal theft by friends, relatives, fellow workers or strangers, of wallets, purses or mail, or fraudulent address changes."

It can also happen if people are sloppy. Some people are sloppy about their own genealogical data, and some are sloppy and inconsiderate about protecting that of others. However, the truth is actually worse than that. Anyone can find out just about anything about you if they want to and if they try hard enough.

Now, I don't want to receive a lot of hate mail this week. I'm just stating facts, and I offer this week's "Along Those Lines . . ." column for your consideration and your thoughtful discussion with your family and friends. I hope you'll take a hard look at your genealogical methods and practices and weigh them against some of the basic ways that identity theft can occur.

Ways to Protect Yourself and Your Family's Data

The attentive citizen will take the time to assess his or her vulnerability to identity theft and/or fraud. Here are the most important ways to protect your identity and the information about other family members.

Change Your Question and/or Answer

Anyone wishing to learn a woman's mother's maiden name can easily find that at the courthouse by accessing a marriage record. If someone knows where you went to school, they can request a transcript of your records or, even easier, go look at the yearbooks in the library. Many companies recognize that the old question about your mother's maiden name can be an Achilles heel for security. Some are offering alternate questions, such as "What was your first pet's name?" or some other question. I have taken the initiative to contact banks and other entities using the "maiden name" question and have asked for another question. Those that don't have an alternative question have, on presentation of proper identity, all allowed me to change the maiden name to another name I chose. (It's the combination of two maiden names of other, much older generations, and it would take a Cray supercomputer to crack the code, I suspect.)

Always Privatize the Files You Share with Others

Most of us share computer files with other researchers. If you create GEDCOM files and upload them to websites for inclusion in a place like the Ancestry World Tree, WorldConnect, and other locations, you are urged to use your program's "privatize" facility to prevent inclusion of information about living people. Typically, living persons' names, their dates, and all other details are excluded— or some generic comment about LIVING is substituted.

Maintain Two Databases or Consider Excluding Living People from Your Database

A friend of mine has been using the Family Tree Maker software for more than a decade. He actually maintains two files: one includes the current and previous generations of his family in which there are living persons; the other includes all the deceased ancestors and their lines. He works with each file separately, which requires him to group materials and plan his data entry work a little more carefully. When he wants to combine the data to produce reports, he simply creates a backup version of each file with different names, and then merges them together. When he wants to share information with others or upload a GEDCOM to a website database, he only shares what he calls "the dead people's file." If someone contacts him for the living generations, he qualifies the person before he shares any data.

Exercise Confidentiality with Others and Demand It of Them

Citing a source in your notes that indicates that a piece of evidence came from "E-mail received from Mary Lou Jones at mary1@superdupernet.com on 11 July 1999" may look good, but it may not take you out of legal harm's way if your own file contains data provided by someone else. The fact that you acted as a conduit for some piece of data used by a person who used it to create a fraudulent identity used in the commission of a criminal act MIGHT just make you an accessory before the fact. Ouch! (I don't want to work on my genealogy from the state prison.)

You Might Consider What Several Genealogists Have Done

Don't share information on a living individual without obtaining a signed document from the intended recipient agreeing not to share the data in any way with anyone without your prior written permission. An e-mail to that effect has little force in a court of law, but a signed agreement does. As for yourself, I suggest that you use caution and consideration when using any data received from another researcher.

Store Important Documents in a Secure Place

This applies not only to your current identity and financial materials, but also to those genealogical documents that might provide a path to a house burglar to other records—even to creating an identity.

Never Carry Original Identity Materials with You If You Don't Have To
Yes, you need your driver's license to drive, but you sure don't need your Social Security card. How often do you use it? Typically you only need it when applying for a job or when opening a financial account where taxes will be reported. In fact, it is against the law in many states for a retailer to ask for a social security number as a form of identification for a check. Similarly, you probably only use your voter registration card for identification at the polls on election day. There's no need to carry these items with you. But if you feel you must, make a photocopy to keep with you. Leave the original in a safe place at home or in the safe deposit box at the bank.

Prepare a List of All Your Credit Cards and Identifications
If you've ever lost your wallet or purse and had to locate all the information that needed to be replaced or credit cards cancelled, you know how important this little piece of advance work can be. Prepare a list of institution or organization, a descriptor of the item from them, the number/expiration date, and a local or toll-free telephone number. Make two copies of the document. One should be stored in a secure place at home where you can quickly locate it. Another copy should be stored in a safe deposit box. Keep it updated. Don't forget driver's license, passport, birth certificate, visas, and other items.

Request a Credit Report At Least Annually
The fastest way to catch fraudulent financial activity is to request a credit report at least once a year. The report helps you keep tabs on your credit status, it identifies any discrepancies caused be errors in reporting or fraudulent activity.

What to Do If You Become a Victim
Identity theft became a federal crime in 1998, and forty-seven states have since passed their own anti-identity theft legislation to protect their citizens. If you become aware of an attempt to use your identity or your resources for any purpose whatsoever, immediately report it to the police. The local police will help decide who at the state or

federal level might need to be called in. You want to limit your personal liability for any damages, and you also want to be able to provide all the information you can to stop the fraudulent activity.

The best deterrent is, of course, preventative action. I am a proponent of sharing genealogical information with others, but I also know there are risks associated with that. Some people have blatantly "stolen" data I uploaded as a GEDCOM file and are passing it off as their own. A few have also posted information on living members of their own families in addition to the information I had privatized. Thank goodness that I paid attention to that detail because they sure don't care.

Be thoughtful and responsible. Consider the content of your data before you share it, and privatize it to protect yourself and other family members. And be mindful of the data you share on all levels. You really CAN prevent yourself from become a victim of identity theft.

Happy Hunting!

George

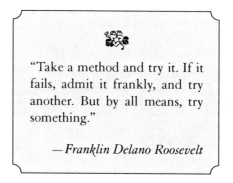

"Take a method and try it. If it fails, admit it frankly, and try another. But by all means, try something."

— *Franklin Delano Roosevelt*

Featured Columnists

The Secret Professionals Don't Share
2 May 2002
Patricia Law Hatcher, CG, FASG

THERE IS A SECRET FOR SUCCESSFUL RESEARCH that professional genealogists don't share with others. Before I am deluged with complaints from my professional friends and colleagues, let me say up front that they don't deliberately withhold the secret. In fact, they don't even know it is a secret. It is so ingrained in how they work, that they probably have never even thought about it.

What is this secret? The research report. "Aargh!" I hear you cry, "I don't want to write a report." It is, however, the secret to organizing your research process effectively. Examples of research reports have been presented in several books and manuals (such as the "BCG Genealogical Standards Manual") and in syllabus material at conferences. The core of the secret lies not so much in the details of presentation, but in the typical sections of a research report:

- Assignment
- Information provided by client and prior reports
- Sources searched

- Findings and analysis
- Suggestions for further research

This doesn't necessarily look like it applies to your research—or does it? Let's look at this item by item. As we do so, we'll examine each with the family historian in mind.

The section is labeled "Assignment," but professionals most often receive from the client what are better called "Goals," such as "Identify parents and spouse of John Jones." Sound familiar? This goal is, however, far too broad to be a practical assignment. It is best to make the goal more bite size. The solution might be to break the search for the parents apart from the search for a spouse, but that often isn't the most effective way to research.

Instead, be practical. Consider breaking the goal down by record groups and/or by repository. For example, "Search census records at NARA branch for Jones and collateral families in Green County."

In a professional report, there is usually a subheading within the assignment that defines the time limitation. I would suggest that you begin by thinking in approximate four-hour chunks.

Open a new file in your word processor. Create a heading for "Immediate goal" and then state your goal. Follow this with a heading for "Projected time" and put "4 hours."

The professional works based on information provided by the client and any prior reports. What do you know about your problem? At this point you may cry, "But I have LOTS of stuff." Maybe it isn't as much as you think. The research report forces the professional to focus. He or she focuses on facts, not hypothesis. The professional also knows to focus on what is pertinent to this portion of the problem.

When I focus only on pertinent facts, I have seen dozens of sheets of paper sent by clients collapse to three statements of records found and two statements of records searched unsuccessfully. Notice the latter category. Do not neglect to state it as part of what you know. It either tells you something important about your ancestors, or it tells you that the method used for searching may have been deficient.

We're going to digress here for a reality check. At this point in preparing a client report—or in picking up on old research of my own—I often find that I have no business proceeding with my stated goal because the data that I already have is defective. For example, I may find that I can't search for collateral lines because I know the names of the siblings but they have no spouses identified.

Or there is a deed of sale listed, but no deed of purchase. Were all the deeds searched? I can't tell. Or the 1850 census abstract for the young William Wilson family fails to list neighbors, so I won't know which of the two dozen Wilson families in the county I should be considering.

When this happens, I usually end up redefining the most urgent research goal. Once I've got the correct goal, it's time to make a Research Plan. Before leaving home, I outline what sources I will check, in what order. With many catalogs now available online, I often enter full citations—with call numbers—and print the list before leaving home.

The Research Plan doesn't appear in a typical report because it is hidden. Or, more accurately, it morphs from "Sources to search" to "Sources searched."

As I research, I note my findings in writing—including negative results.

Too many family researchers consider the research results as the final step of the process. The secret, however, lies in the analysis of those findings (both specific and general) and in the last section of the report, "Suggestions for further research."

Both the analysis and the suggestions should always be written out. It makes it easier to share with others and is immensely helpful if we must put a project aside for a while.

The suggestions should be written as an itemized list. Each suggestion might be a research goal, but you can't do everything at once. With the future research suggestions clearly listed, it is easier to focus and to prioritize your next goal. The list also reduces the possibility that you may overlook a potentially productive research path.

Is the Record Wrong? —Likely Mistakes
16 May 2002
Patricia Law Hatcher, CG, FASG,

IT'S A QUANDARY WE OCCASIONALLY FACE in genealogy—a record that "just doesn't fit" or conflicts with other data. Or perhaps it's a name or fact for which we can find no other records. Is it possible that the record is wrong?

In my conversations with other serious researchers, I find some who are more willing than I am to say that a record is wrong. I hesitate to proclaim that a record is in error unless I believe that it is a LIKELY error. What are likely errors?

The Echo Syndrome
One of the most common errors is what I describe as an echo. Let's say that the birth record of your ancestor reads, "Constance, dau. of John & Constance Jones, b. 17 May 1777." So you look and look for a marriage of John Jones to a Constance in the appropriate time period. There is nothing.

To determine if a record error is likely or not, it is necessary first to look at the record in context. You return to the vital records. John and Constance had no other children. However, there are several births for children of John and Alice. When you examine them as a group, the likely error is readily apparent.

- Alice, dau. of John & Alice Jones, b. 7 March 1773
- Barbara, dau. of John & Alice Jones, b. 20 April 1775
- Constance, dau. of John & Constance Jones, b. 17 May 1777
- Deliverance, dau. of John & Alice Jones, b. 23 April 1779
- Elizabeth, dau. of John & Alice Jones, b. 13 June 1780
- Faith, dau. of John & Alice Jones, b. 9 February 1783

A common mistake is to record the name of one person as that of another person who was involved in the event. In this case, the mother's name echoes that of the daughter.

Second-Class Persons

Men were considered more important than women and children. In addition, the recorder was more likely to know the men in the community personally than to know the women or children. Therefore, errors are more likely to be made in the names of women than of men.

Census Echoes

We very often see echoes in the place of birth on censuses. There are a variety of reasons, ranging from laziness or lack of precision on the part of the enumerator to the reluctance of the enumerated to impart any information that was not directly requested. Once again, the errors are more likely to occur in the information about women and children. When the wife's state of birth is the same as that of her husband (or the husband's birth state is the same as where they are living), I always feel safer with a second record confirming it before I pursue further research.

For example, in 1880 the census taker visited a household in which lived a widow and four of her grown children. For all five, the enumerated noted the place of birth of the individual and parents as LA LA LA. In 1850 and 1860, however, the husband and father had given his state of birth as TN. Clearly, the enumerator had echoed the information for the widow as also being that of her children. (Hint: To avoid this trap, check to see what all siblings said in 1880 and later. The results don't necessarily agree with each other, which points out how important this extra step is.)

Failure to Ask

The census taker was counting people in the Fred and Margaret Smith household; he was not recording vital events. So he probably asked, "What are the names of the children and how old are they?" to which the answer—an accurate one—was "Able is 8, Barbary is 6, and Charles is 3." He then carefully recorded "Able Smith 8, Barbary Smith 6, and Charles Smith 3." The only problem for descendants is that Able and Barbary were the children of Margaret's first marriage, to John Jones.

It is likely that names in blended households could be recorded erroneously. This, in turn, might cause the researcher to look for a marriage for father Fred and mother Margaret preceding the birth of Able, rather than that of Charles. Or, if a marriage is found for Fred Smith and Margaret Jones, the conclusion would be that Fred had a first wife and the doomed search would begin for the Jones parents of Margaret.

Old Habits Die Hard

I shouldn't have much difficulty convincing you of this likely error. How many checks did you date January 2001 earlier this year? (Hint: I write the new year in advance on the first dozen or so checks to avoid this problem!) Ministers, clerks, and justices of the peace were human beings. They did the same thing.

Check the original in context. If the events were recorded in chronological order, you may be able to demonstrate the error by showing that it is chronologically impossible to record a child born in January 1822 immediately after a child born in December 1822. If, however, the events are recorded in family-record format and say that John was born in August 1821 and Jane was born in January 1822, you'll just have to explain that it is MORE likely that Jane's birth was recorded erroneously and was really January 1823 and LESS likely that John was really born in 1820 and his birth year recorded incorrectly.

How Likely Is It?
We must always be careful not to overlay modern values on people who lived one or more centuries before us. On the other hand, certain human traits are not modern inventions. When a record becomes problematic, consult the original. Make sure that your notes accurately reflect what it says. Then analyze the record to see if there is a potential "likely error."

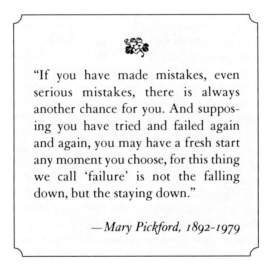

"If you have made mistakes, even serious mistakes, there is always another chance for you. And supposing you have tried and failed again and again, you may have a fresh start any moment you choose, for this thing we call 'failure' is not the falling down, but the staying down."

—*Mary Pickford, 1892-1979*

Likely and Unlikely Mistakes
30 May 2002
Patricia Law Hatcher, CG, FASG

AN EARLIER ARTICLE EXPOSED JUST THE TIP OF THE ICEBERG, so to speak, on the issue of likely mistakes in original records. (See<http://www.ancestry.com/rd/prodredir.asp?sourceid=831&key=A575801>.)This article looks at some other things to consider in analyzing possible mistakes.

Absent-minded Clerics
Some ministers did not immediately record the events they performed. This was especially true when the baptism, marriage, or burial was performed at some distance from the church. In many cases, the minister probably assumed he would remember to record the events upon his return. (How often have you not bothered to write down an appointment, sure that you'll remember to put it on the calendar when you get home?) In reality, it may be the crumpled note, "wedding at Sam Smith's," found in a coat pocket weeks later that reminded him. What would he forget or remember incorrectly? The date? Or that the bride was not Sam's sister, but his sister-in-law, Tabitha True?

How can you tell if you have an absent-minded recorder? You can't, but the original record may hold clues. Are events recorded chronologically as they occurred or are several out of sequence? Do the ink and handwriting suggest that events were recorded in clumps? Are there blanks in any of the records (not necessarily the one for your ancestor)?

I had a problem in which the month and year matched between a birth record and a tombstone, but the given name was blank on the birth record and the day was different. I'm never surprised when the year doesn't match, but I expect the month and day to be the same. Did I have the wrong record? I reexamined the original and noticed that the next event, which appeared to have been recorded at the same sitting had even more blank spaces. It seemed likely that the minister not only could not remember several facts, he had remembered the day of the birth incorrectly.

Off a Line

Did you ever have to stay after school and write "I will not talk in class" fifty or 100 or even 500 times? I did. A lot. From experience I can tell you that if I didn't use lined paper, the last line on the page was significantly off the horizontal. The same was true of scribes of the past.

Consider a list of marriages with columns for groom, bride, date, and official. Very often, they don't line up as well as we would like. If any fields are blank, the potential for confusion is worse. Some records are spread across two pages—and perhaps microfilmed as separate sheets. If you are having difficulty with a record from a tabular format, carefully reexamine the original. The mistake might lie with you or the abstractor, rather than the original record.

Pre-1850 censuses are fraught with danger because they have both rows and columns that can be difficult to keep straight. If you find yourself having difficulty matching a family with the age brackets on an early census, stop immediately and reread the microfilm. You may find that the problem lies with your notes. The extra column for males sixteen to eighteen on the 1820 is a potential pitfall. (Hint: The column for youngest females usually has numbers on almost every line. I use it to assure myself that my counts are correctly oriented.)

In tabular information, although the recorder may have gotten "off," perhaps by omitting some data, it is more likely that the mistake occurred in copying the entry instead.

Repetitive Mistakes

How many times might the same mistake occur in the record? While it is easy to make a slip once, it is much less likely for it to occur multiple times. Thus, if a deed mentions a name three times in different places, it is not as likely that the name is in error as if it only occurred once in the deed.

Unlikely Mistakes

Interestingly, the concept of LIKELY mistakes has a flip side—that of UNlikely mistakes. Sometimes, when we have two conflicting pieces of information, we would do well to ask ourselves which of the potential errors is more UNlikely.

For example, suppose that the 1920 census proclaims that your ancestor Elizabeth was born in 1854. However, you find Elizabeth listed as a two-year-old on the 1850 census. Doesn't it seem UNlikely (in fact, impossible) that the census taker prognosticated her birth? It also seems UNlikely (albeit not impossible) that the child died and that the next-born girl was given the name of the deceased child—especially in this time period.

On the other hand, how likely is it that your ancestor—either accidentally or deliberately—became younger as she grew older? Quite frankly, the older you get, the less important it seems to be to remember your exact age. I know—I always have to do the math to respond to the question, "How old are you?"

But suppose your ancestor Elizabeth's death certificate in 1932 says she was seventy-eight at her death? Is the 1850 census outvoted? Of course not. The death certificate information was provided by someone other than Elizabeth. The provider was dependent upon Elizabeth or another source, and furthermore was relying on his or her own memory. (Which reminds me—I need to call my son and find out which day this month is my daughter-in-law's birthday. I never can remember.)

In the previous article, we discussed the "echo" syndrome in census birthplaces. So let's talk about the flip side. Suppose that in 1870 the birth places for Tom and his wife Fanny are both given as MS, but the 1880 household for three widowed women imparts the following information:

- Dolly, head, 70, GA, GA, GA
- Elizabeth, daughter, 50, MS, GA, SC
- Fanny, granddaughter, 30, TX, MS, LA

Where was Fanny born? Clearly, we're not seeing any echo in 1880, although it is a possibility in 1870. The information in 1880 is internally consistent (Fanny's mother born MS; Elizabeth's mother born GA). Furthermore, the individuals intimately involved in the events (Dolly in the birth of Elizabeth, Elizabeth in the birth of Fanny) are all present in the household. Do you think it is likely Fanny was born in MS and unlikely that she was born in TX—or vice versa?

Ask Yourself—Likely or Unlikely?

When you are faced with problematic records, analyze them in their full context, make sure the mistake is not in the abstract rather than the original, and then ask yourself which information is LIKELY to be a mistake and which is UNlikely to be a mistake.

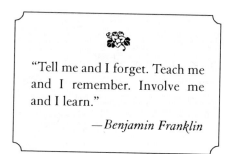

"Tell me and I forget. Teach me and I remember. Involve me and I learn."

—*Benjamin Franklin*

Pallot's Index, 1780 to 1837: Part I, Disk Version
7 May 2002
Sherry Irvine, CGRS, FSA (Scot)

PALLOT'S INDEX HAD ITS BEGINNINGS in the early 1800s, with the creation of an English firm of heir searchers. Subsequently it became the property of Messrs Pallot and Co., who gave the index its name. Today, Pallot's Index belongs to the Institute of Heraldic and Genealogical Studies at Canterbury, Kent. They made it available for consultation at their library or allowed searches for a fee. Recently, Ancestry.com has joined with the Institute to produce the index on CD-ROM and offer it through the Ancestry.com databases online.

At one time, Pallot's Index was much larger. Unfortunately, it suffered severe damage during World War II. What survives is roughly 1.7 million references to marriages and 200,000 references to births. It is the marriages that are most useful for London and its environs in particular; there are entries for 101 of the 103 ancient parishes. For county marriages, thirty-eight counties are represented, and for nine of the counties, more than one hundred parishes are represented in the index: Cornwall, Gloucestershire, Hampshire, Leicestershire, Middlesex/London, Norfolk, Nottinghamshire, Shropshire, and Somerset. Yorkshire is close behind with ninety-three. Less than half of the parishes appear tp have been indexed for the full fifty-seven years, most are 1790 to 1812.

Before you begin, read the booklet that comes with the CD and then turn to the Ancestry View "Help" feature for other questions. A basic search is simple—mainly a matter of entering a surname in the field at the top of the screen and selecting "Go." At the lower right is displayed the total number of hits on view. Work your way through them by clicking on "Next" in the toolbar at the top and watch the numbers advance. You can put in name variants one by one or make use of wild card symbols.

In the simple marriage search, pay attention to the display of results because listings for the targeted name do not necessarily come first. The place of those listings is wherever they fit in alphabetical order for all results that match the search criteria (e.g., a request for marriage entries of people named Worthington will first show surnames of spouses beginning with letters A through V). In addition, my experiments with several names show there is not necessarily a complete duplication of entries—checking only those within the list of individuals with the selected surname may not find every event.

I recommend using the advanced search option because of several added features. There is the advantage of adding more facts (parents or spouse's name, place, year) and of viewing the flow chart of results. The best way to explain this is with an example. Put in Smith alone and there are over 51,000 names; Baker nets about 8400. Enter "Smith and Baker" in the surname field, and you will see how many thousands of each surname are in the database. The two names appear together 125 times. Add a first name or names and the numbers drop even more. The beauty of this system is that you watch a diagrammatic representation of any combination of fields. In addition, you can look for only first names—there is no requirement to input a surname, a real asset when the first name is unusual.

Another feature is the ability to browse the entries of one parish; enter a place name in the parish field and leave the others blank. For some large urban parishes there are tens of thousands, but for others, such as Swyre in Dorset (not in the IGI) there are just 112 marriages. The computer does not group records; you must use the "Next" button to advance through the hits. To narrow the search, you can combine the parish name with a specific year but not a range of years. This inability to search by year range is a shortcoming; however, as an alternative, you can tag and print entries of interest.

Every record display looks the same, the name of child or spouse No.1, name of parents or spouse No. 2, date and parish name. At the top, if you are hooked up to the Internet, it is possible to select "Check here to view this image online."

As you search, watch what happens in the source window on the left. All you see at first is a list of letters of the alphabet with numbers, plus signs and boxes beside them. The numbers indicate how the hits are distributed through the alphabet. Select a plus sign and you see the surnames involved; click on a name to go to that entry. Check a box and it is possible to print a list of all the entries for that surname.

Pallot's Indexes to marriages and baptisms are also accessible through a subscription to Ancestry's UK/Ireland Collection <http://www.ancestry.com/rd/redir.asp?sourceid=831&targetid=3345>. Search techniques are quite different and will be discussed in another article.

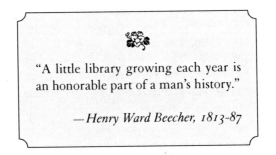

"A little library growing each year is an honorable part of a man's history."

—*Henry Ward Beecher, 1813-87*

Pallot's Index, 1780 to 1837: Part 2, Web Version
21 May 2002
Sherry Irvine, BA, CGRS, FSA (Scot)

PALLOT'S INDEX CONTAINS REFERENCES to marriages and baptisms in England and Wales, 1780 to 1847. There are more than 1.5 million marriage events and about 200,000 baptisms within the two parts. When targeting Pallot's data through the website, the marriages and baptisms are searched separately.

A free search from the home page will indicate whether the name of interest appears in Pallot's Index. Subscribers can select this and be taken directly to the basic search screen for the index. Or they can access the index, whether baptisms or marriages, by following these steps:

At the home page select the "Search Records" tab.

Next, select "UK & Ireland" and then click on England (on the map).

A list of databases for England is available on this page. Advance to the Pallot's Index listings and select the one you require. This advanced search has seven fields for marriage searches and nine for baptisms. Many records are incomplete, although occasionally there is additional information such as an occupation.

- Individual Given Name/Child's Given Name
- Child's Middle Name (baptisms only)
- Individual Surname/Child's Surname
- Spouse First Name/Father's Name
- Spouse Last Name/Mother's Name
- Parish
- County (baptisms only)
- Marriage Date/Baptism Date (range of years not possible)
- Keyword

The Help option ("?" at the end of the navigation bar} near the top of the screen is there to be used. (When did you last read the information about search techniques?)

The system supports Soundex codes and the usual wild card symbols: "?" for a single letter, "*" for 0 to 6 letters and "**" for 0 to more than six letters. When using any of these, note that the first three letters of a name must be included. Test some examples of your own, or these:

R?der is not a permitted search but Rayb?rn is

Thom*son finds Thomson and Thompson

Roberts* finds Roberts, Robertson

War**n finds Warrington, as well as Warburton, Warden, Warren, etc.

Note: There are limitations on wildcard searches as to how many matches they will return, so it is best to put in as much information as possible and rotate in some of the variables, rather than leaving too many characters out.

The various fields and input options together provide plenty of scope for name variants and checking locations. In addition, the search can be by parish name only, by parish name and year, or by first name only. Linkages are also possible, i.e., combining one or two names with a parish and/or a date; or combining a full name of one spouse with just the first name of the other.

The parish name-only search should reveal whether your parish or parishes are part of the index. This is not a certainty because county names, particularly with marriages, do not always accompany the names of parishes outside of London, and when they do they are in numerous short forms. Where there is only the dedication of the church, e.g., St. Anne, it is predominantly for London churches. Enter Masham, which is in the North Riding of Yorkshire, and the results are 1,694 marriages and 3,998 baptisms. There may be slight discrepancies between the totals of the CD and Web versions, probably related to the prevalence of incomplete entries.

The one drawback to the enhanced search is returning to it. The results page or pages do not include a link. If you have looked at several pages of results, it is necessary to select the "more info" option at the bottom and choose "Go to the enhanced search template." It would be a nice improvement to have an option for a direct return to the enhanced search.

Results from marriage and baptism searches are presented in alphabetical order; facts include names of parties to a marriage or names of child and parents, the date of the event and the location. Off to the right is the icon, which takes you to the image of the original index entry. At the top of the display page is a link to a printer friendly version of the list of results.

The style of the results display of the Web version is, for me, preferable to CD system where you must use the "next" button to jump from one result to the next and then tag all interesting records in order to bring them together. On the other hand, the Ancestry View system on the CD offers the search option diagram and a scrollable list of all words in the database (see Part One). Admittedly, odd words can be found using the online form of Pallot's by entering a term in the keyword field, but the CD diagram is a wonderful feature. If you happen to be interested in odd entries, in the marriage index, try inputting "discontin*." (A few individuals evidently got cold feet.)

This series will conclude with a third part, on using the data. Note: Access to Pallot's Birth and Marriage Indexes are available with a subscription to the UK and Ireland Collection. To subscribe, go to <http://www.ancestry.com/rd/redir.asp?sourceid=831& targetid=3345>.

The Custom of Naming Children
9 May 2002
Karen Frisch

LONG BEFORE CHILDREN'S NAMES were chosen for their beauty or popularity, parents had other criteria for selecting names. Names were chosen not for their originality but often to honor relatives, either dead or living. Consequently the same names tended to be repeated through successive generations in European countries as well as in Jewish and Chinese tradition.

For centuries naming children after family members has been a common practice. If a name cuts across several generations, including cousins, it usually indicates a family connection.

The desire to perpetuate names is so strong that parents in the late 1700s and early 1800s took steps to ensure that a name did not die out even if the child did. Early American records contain listings of a child being given the same name as a sibling who had died previously. The result is the appearance of a "Kent Wheeler 2d," who appears in birth records for 1777, named after his brother by the same name who was born in 1771 but died prematurely. Kent was their maternal grandmother's surname.

Repetition of names is helpful to the modern-day genealogist

intent on determining family relationships. On occasion a child will
be given the complete name of a family elder, as in the case of Israel
Whitaker Drowne, born in 1810, when his father named him after
his own grandfather who was born one hundred years earlier in
1710. Such a custom is evidence of considerable respect or affection
within families.

Surnames arose in the Middle Ages out of necessity to differen-
tiate individuals with the same first name. They were also a way to
acknowledge the occupation of the person—Miller or Cartwright,
for example.

Both first and last names often became Anglicized once a family came to America. A name that originated as Margarethe in
Germany, was often changed to Margaret two generations later
when her namesake was born in America.

Daughters were named after their mothers just as sons were for
their fathers. One family found among their ancestors eleven family members over seven decades who were given some combination
of the names Henrietta, Ernestine, and Augusta to honor the family matriarch and her daughters, who were born in the 1860s.

With the tradition of reversing or varying names through different generations, family relationships become easier to spot in the
record books. It gets confusing, however, when the desire to bestow
an honored name upon someone results in cousins who were born
in the same town being given the same name—especially when they
both marry women named Mary two years apart. In such a situation genealogists are forced to depend on other records to determine Mary's correct surname. Children named after maternal relatives can also help to distinguish the two lines.

During America's colonial period families also favored names
based on virtues. Patience, Mercy, Benevolence, Thankful,
Deliverance, and even Experience are on record. They were usually given to women, but not exclusively. Such names were often
paired with a short last name, as in the case of Experience White.

Military leaders under whom soldiers served frequently appear
as children's names following the Revolutionary War and the War
of 1812. The names Bertha and Betsey are repeated over generations in the Drowne family until in 1817 the name Tower begins to

appear as a middle name. Betsey's grandfather fought in the Revolution under Captain Levi Tower.

A George Washington Smith who appears in birth records from 1809 reflects two things: a patriotism at the turn of the new century and a distinctive first name giving emphasis to the most common surname. If you find yourself playing the name game with your ancestors, knowledge of family names can offer helpful clues.

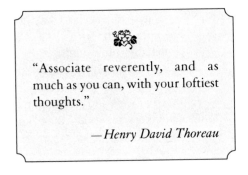

"Associate reverently, and as much as you can, with your loftiest thoughts."

— *Henry David Thoreau*

A Military Hero of a Different Sort
23 May 2002
Megan Smolenyak

Andrew Carroll never ceases to amaze me. For those of you who may not be familiar with him, he is the founder and director of The Legacy Project that "works to honor and remember those who have served this nation in wartime by seeking out and saving their letters."

Not content to publish the bestseller, *War Letters: Extraordinary Correspondence from American Wars,* and donate all his earnings from the book to veterans groups, Andrew has launched a new initiative to give away two million copies of *War Letters* to active and retired military personnel and is currently on a cross-country road trip as part of this effort. I'll share more details about this undertaking, but first, I'd like to share what motivates Andrew. Here, in his own words, is his story.

The Battle to Preserve War Letters
I had no particular interest in history or letters until a fire swept through my family's home in Washington, D.C., just before Christmas of 1989. Thankfully, no one was hurt (even Claude, our cat, bounded out safely), but all our possessions were destroyed. As

I walked cautiously through the burnt-out shell of our house several days later, it suddenly occurred to me that all my letters were gone. The clothes, the furniture, the books, just about everything else could be replaced, but not the letters.

There was certainly nothing worthy of the National Archives, mostly just correspondences with old girlfriends and high school buddies traveling abroad. But I did have a series of riveting letters by a friend who was in Beijing during the Tiananmen Square massacre in June 1989. It was crushing to realize that his letters, along with the seemingly trivial ones, were now gone.

The fire—which, in retrospect was something of a godsend—inspired in me a lifelong passion for letters. And ultimately it triggered the creation of the Legacy Project, a national nonprofit organization I founded in 1998 that encourages Americans to seek out and preserve their family correspondence.

Our focus on war began after I spoke with a handful of veterans who said that they had thrown away their old letters. They were very modest about their service and felt no one would be interested in what they had written. Even more tragically, I discovered that over a thousand veterans were dying a day, and their loved ones were often discarding their letters as well. This was stunning to me. The few war letters I had seen were more emotionally intense and dramatic than anything I had ever read. Composed under life and death circumstances, every letter took on new meaning. Soldiers never knew if that letter would be their last, which often inspired in them greater clarity and poetry of expression. "You don't mince words in a foxhole," one veteran explained to me.

On a whim, I contacted "Dear Abby" and asked her to write a column urging her readers to save their war letters and, if they thought they had something historically significant, to send a photocopy to the Legacy Project. "Dear Abby" agreed, and the column appeared on 11 November 1998—Veterans Day.

Three days later, the post office called. "Is this Andrew Carroll?" a clerk asked testily. I said it was. "You need to come down here now and get your mail." I assured the clerk that I would hop on my bike and be there in minutes. "Bring a car," he said, and hung up. He wasn't kidding.

Bins and bins of letters were pouring in. I immediately tore into the envelopes and began reading. Here were eyewitness accounts of Gettysburg and D-Day, Shiloh and Pearl Harbor, the Tet Offensive, Desert Storm, St. Mihiel, and even e-mails from Bosnia. Every war in our nation's history was represented.

I was only three years old when U.S. troops pulled out of Vietnam in 1973, and no one in my immediate family has ever served in the armed forces. Nothing I had ever seen, or read, or been told about war prepared me for what I received. I had braced myself for graphic descriptions of bloodshed and stories of brutality and suffering, and I suspected there would be intimate letters to wives and girlfriends written by forlorn soldiers who, in so many cases, later died in battle. What caught me off guard were the personal messages enclosed with every war letter sent to me:

"Dear Sir, Please accept these letters that my brother had written to my mother. My brother is missing (not a POW). He was never right after he returned home and one day he was just gone. I hope to make his life worth something. I miss him very much."

"I am a widow 85 years old and my husband and only son have passed. My husband served in Patton's Third Army. There is no one I can give these my husband's letters to so you may have them. Please remember him."

Please remember him. Time and time again, the writers pleaded with me to please remember.

Featuring two hundred of the more than 50,000 letters the Legacy Project has received to date, *War Letters: Extraordinary Correspondence from American Wars* was born. Because we had promised that the Legacy Project would not profit from the letters sent, all of my earnings from the book are being donated to veterans groups.

We continue to solicit more letters and will eventually create a Web-based archive and distribute some of the original letters to appropriate museums and collections. Our true mission, though, is to prevent the disposal of this great, unknown literature of the American people. Please remember and acknowledge the veterans in your family or local community by protecting their letters or donating them to a reputable museum, archive, library, or historical society so that future generations will have access to and can learn from these irreplaceable documents. Together, we can keep these letters—which are truly the pages of our national autobiography—from disappearing forever.

The Armed Services Edition

As I mentioned earlier, Andrew recently launched a new initiative by taking a page from the past. In partnership with Washington Square Press (a division of Simon & Schuster) and the Veterans of Foreign Wars (VFW), the Legacy Project recently announced the publication of the first Armed Services Edition (ASE) in fifty-five years. An ASE is a special version of a book, produced specifically to be given to veterans and active military personnel. Over 123 million were given away in the 1940s before they were discontinued in 1947. Andrew collects them and had wanted to bring back this idea for years.

Two million ASE versions of *War Letters* are now in the process of being distributed. Most will be sent by the VFW through the mail to veterans and family members of military personnel, but Andrew is also spending most of May and June traveling across the country handing out thousands of free copies on military bases. Once again, this is being done through Andrew's own money and private donations. He hopes to inspire the publication of other ASE versions of appropriate books such as *Flags of Our Fathers, D-Day,* and *Black Hawk Down.*

What You Can Do

As Memorial Day approaches, what better time to follow Andrew's lead by reflecting on the contributions of our military and making the commitment to honor those who have served? If you would like to learn how to preserve your own family's war letters or donate them to The Legacy Project, or simply want to know more about this remarkable ASE initiative, please visit The Legacy Project's website at <http://www.warletters.com>.

Help Bring Our Korean War Soldiers Home
23 May 2002
Megan Smolenyak

This article originally ran in May 2001, and with the upcoming Memorial Day holiday looming, it is appropriate that we re-run it.

When I spoke with Megan at the NGS Conference in Milwaukee, she told me the California legislation that threatens to severely restrict access to vital records indexes in California will make her work on this project much more difficult. For more information on California Senate Bill 1614, and contact information for California legislators, go to <http://www.ancestry. com/rd/prodredir.asp?sourceid=831&key=A577701>.

Juliana Smith
Editor, Ancestry Daily News

BALTIMORE PAYNE WAS BORN IN 1912 in Illinois to parents who had ventured slightly north from Missouri. He was one of ten children and grew up to marry, have children, and join the Army. In 1950, he was sent to Korea where he paid the ultimate price, dying just as most Americans were celebrating Thanksgiving. Unfortunately, the circumstances of his death were such that his remains were never found, so his family was denied the chance to pay their respects, bury him, and properly grieve.

The U.S. Army's Repatriation and Family Affairs Division—which recently traced his family to people with five surnames residing in four states—is working to change that. The objective of this organization is to locate and re-establish ties with the family members of the 6,318 soldiers who were never accounted for in the Korean War. To put this into perspective, this is about three times as many soldiers as those still unaccounted for from Vietnam. The ticking clock—fifty years and counting—makes it both urgent and somewhat difficult to find these soldiers' families.

By locating family members, the Army hopes not only to help with the inevitable, unanswered questions, but also to build a database of mitochondrial DNA (mtDNA) samples. With relations with North Korea slowly improving (this, in spite of the fact that an official cessation of hostilities was never declared!) and search and recovery efforts escalating, the Army has more hope of bringing soldiers home now than they did in the first four decades following the war. During the 1990s, several hundred sets of remains were repatriated, but now the challenge is to identify them so they can be accorded a formal military funeral.

At this point, approximately thirty percent of the soldiers' families have been found and the mtDNA database contains samples for slightly more than twenty percent of the soldiers. As the database grows, so do the chances of matches confirming the identification of Baltimore Payne or any individual missing soldier.

The Army would like your help in finding the other 4,000+ families. Please don't think you can't help just because you weren't even born then. Almost everyone in the U.S. knows of someone who served in Korea, whether he returned or not. Maybe it was your grandfather or your brother. Maybe it was that acquaintance from high school. Maybe it was that fellow who worked at the mill with your father. Or maybe it was you.

If you have any connection—no matter how remote—to anyone who served in Korea, please visit <http://www.koreanwar.org>.

This site lists all the men who are still unaccounted for. You can search for a soldier's name and then leave a remembrance with whatever details you might have. No detail is too insignificant, but ones pertaining to the soldiers' families are especially helpful.

Names of siblings (generally not contained in the soldiers' files) can often bring a case to resolution. A remarriage of the soldier's mother or the fact that his brood moved from New Jersey to Arizona can be enormously useful. Just think for yourself what information you would need to trace a line in your own extended clan forward from 1950. The same information is needed by the Army. Remember, too, that others who served frequently knew quite a lot about the stateside lives of their fellow soldiers. Please consider quizzing any Korean War veterans you might know about the men they served with. Should you note a "DNA" tag next to the soldier's name, this means his family is being actively sought. If you see this, you might want to consider calling the Army directly at 1-800-892-2490 in addition to leaving a remembrance.

Baltimore gave his life for his country. That it happened fifty years ago makes it no smaller a sacrifice or any less important. The Korean War was fought from 1950 to 1953, so we are in the midst of an extended fiftieth anniversary. What more fitting tribute than to see that as many of these soldiers as possible are properly honored and interred?

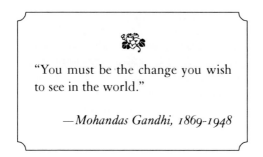

"You must be the change you wish to see in the world."

—*Mohandas Gandhi, 1869-1948*

May 2002
U.S. Record Collection

The following databases are accessible only by Ancestry.com data subscribers.

Ansonia, Derby, Shelton, and Seymour, Connecticut City Directory, 1907 (Images online)
http://www.ancestry.com/rd/prodredir.asp?sourceid=831&key=D6275

This database contains the 1907 city directory for the cities of Ansonia, Derby, Shelton, and Seymour, located in New Haven County, Connecticut. In addition to providing the names of the heads of households, it provides their addresses and occupational information. Also included are a business and street directory, information on local schools, churches, banks, societies, and other miscellaneous information. Images of the original directory accompany this database.

Source Information: Ancestry.com. "Ansonia, Derby, Shelton, and Seymour, Connecticut City Directory, 1907" [database online]. Provo, UT: Ancestry.com, 2002. Original data: "Ansonia, Derby, Shelton, and Seymour Directory 1907: Containing a General Directory of the Citizens, Classified Business Directories, Street Directories, New Map, City Officers, Town Officers, Churches, Schools, Societies, Etc." New Haven, CT: The Price & Lee Company, 1907.

❀

Ansonia, Derby, Shelton, and Seymour, Connecticut City Directory, 1906 (Images online)
http://www.ancestry.com/rd/prodredir.asp?sourceid=831&key=D6294

This database contains the 1906 city directory for the cities of Ansonia, Derby, Shelton, and Seymour located in New Haven County, Connecticut. In addition to providing the names of the heads of households, it provides their addresses and occupational information. Also included are a business and street directory, information on local schools, city and town officers, churches, banks, societies, and other miscellaneous information.

Source Information: Ancestry.com. "Ansonia, Derby, Shelton, and Seymour, Connecticut City Directory, 1906" [database online]. Provo, UT: Ancestry.com, 2002. Original data: "Ansonia, Derby, Shelton, and Seymour, Connecticut City Directory, 1906: Containing a General Directory of the Citizens, Classified Business Directories, Street Directories, New Map, City Officers, Town Officers, Churches, Schools, Societies, Etc." New Haven, CT: The Price & Lee Co., 1906.

❀

Augusta, Farmingdale, Gardiner, Hallowell, and Randolph, Maine City Directory, 1935 (Images online)
http://www.ancestry.com/rd/prodredir.asp?sourceid=831&key=D6291

This database contains the 1935 city directory for the cities of Augusta, Farmingdale, Gardiner, Hallowell, and Randolph located in Kennebec County, Maine. In addition to providing the names of the heads of households, it provides their addresses and occupational information. Also included are a business and street directory, information on local schools, government, churches, banks, societies, and other miscellaneous information. Images of the directory accompany this database.

Source Information: Ancestry.com. "Augusta, Farmingdale, Gardiner, Hallowell, and Randolph, Maine City Directory, 1935" [database online]. Provo, UT: Ancestry.com, 2002. Original data: "Manning's Augusta, Gardiner, Hallowell, Farmingdale, Randolph Maine Directory for the Year Beginning November, 1935." Portland, ME: H.A. Manning Company, 1935.

Bristol, Plainville, and Terryville, Connecticut City Directory 1886-87 (Images online)
http://www.ancestry.com/rd/prodredir.asp?sourceid=831&key=D6285

This database contains the 1886-87 city directory for the cities of Bristol, Plainville, and Terryville located in Hartford County, Connecticut. In addition to providing the names of the heads of households, it provides their addresses and occupational information. Also included are a business and street directory, information on local schools, churches, banks, societies, and other miscellaneous information.

Source Information: Ancestry.com. "Bristol, Plainville and Terryville, Connecticut City Directory, 1886-87" [database online]. Provo, UT: Ancestry.com, 2002. Original data: "Bristol, Plainville and Terryville Directory for 1886-87: Containing a General Directory of the Citizens, Classified Business Directory, Town Officers, Churches, Schools, Societies, Etc." New Haven, CT: Price, Lee & Co., 1886-87.

This database is also included in the 1890 Census Reconstruction Project and can be searched through its main page at <http://www.ancestry.com/search/rectype/census/1890sub/main.htm>.

Bristol, Warren and Barrington, Rhode Island, City Directory, 1884 (Images online)
http://www.ancestry.com/rd/prodredir.asp?sourceid=831&key=D6279
This database contains the 1884 city directory for the cities of Bristol, Warren, and Barrington located in Bristol County, Rhode Island. In addition to providing the names of the heads of households, it provides

their addresses and occupational information. Also included are a business and street directory, information on local schools, churches, banks, societies, and other miscellaneous information.

Bristol was originally part of Plymouth Colony, 1681-86, then Bristol County, Massachusetts. It finally ceded to Rhode Island in 1747. Barrington was originally created in 1717 as Barrington, Massachusetts, then was ceded to Rhode Island in 1747 as part of the town of Warren. A new town was set off from Warren in 1770.

Images of the original directory accompany this database.

Source Information: Ancestry.com. "Bristol, Warren, and Barrington Rhode Island City Directory, 1884" [database online]. Provo, UT: Ancestry.com, 2002. Original data: "The Bristol, Warren, and Barrington Directory, 1884: Comprising a Complete General and Business Directory of Bristol County." Boston, MA: Sampson, Davenport, & Co., 1884.

This database is also included in the 1890 Census Reconstruction Project and can be searched through its main page at <http://www.ancestry.com/search/rectype/census/1890sub/main.htm>.

🐾

Brockton and Bridgewaters, Massachusetts City Directory, 1908 (Images Online)
http://www.ancestry.com/rd/prodredir.asp?sourceid=831&key=D6276

This database contains the 1908 city directory for the cities of Brockton, Bridgewater, and East and West Bridgewater located in Plymouth County, Massachusetts. In addition to providing the names of the heads of households, it provides their addresses and occupational information. Also included are a business and street directory, information on local schools, churches, banks, societies, and other miscellaneous information. Images of the original directory accompany this database.

Source Information: Ancestry.com. "Brockton and Bridgewaters, Massachusetts City Directory, 1908" [database online]. Provo, UT: Ancestry.com, 2002. Original data: "1908 Brockton Including the Towns of Bridgewater, East and

West Bridgewater, Massachusetts Directory of the Inhabitants, Business Firms, Manufacturing Establishments, Institutions, Societies, With Map, House Directory, etc." Boston, MAW.A. Greenough & Co., 1908.

❧

Broome County New York, Leading Citizens, 1800-99
http://www.ancestry.com/rd/prodredir.asp?sourceid=831&key=D6284

This database contains information in regards to the leading citizens of Broome County New York between the years 1800-99. Broome County is located in the southern region of the state. The main three cities consist of Binghamton, Endicott, and Johnson. The following information is included in this database if it has been mentioned in the book: name, birth date, birthplace, parents, grandparents, marriage date, spouse information, children, occupation, education, home residence, church affiliation. This database provides a wealth of information for individuals who have ancestors from the Broome County, New York area.

Source Information: Quakenbush, Patricia, comp. "Broome County New York, Leading Citizens, 1800-99" [database online]. Provo, UT: Ancestry.com, 2002. Original data: Leading Citizens of Broome County New York. "Boston Biographical Review Publishing Company." Cole Library, Carlsbad, CA, 1894.

❧

Brunswick and Topsham Village, Maine City Directory, 1910 (Images online)
http://www.ancestry.com/rd/prodredir.asp?sourceid=831&key=D6295

This database contains the 1910 city directory for the cities of Brunswick and Topsham Village located in Cumberland County, Maine. In addition to providing the names of the heads of households, it provides their addresses and occupational information. Also included are a business and street directory, information on local schools, churches, banks, societies, and other miscellaneous information.

Source Information: Ancestry.com. "Brunswick and Topsham Village, Maine City Directory, 1910" [database online]. Provo, UT: Ancestry.com, 2002. Original data: "Resident and Business Directory of the Town of Brunswick and Topsham Villages With Maps, 1910." Augusta, ME: The Mitchell Publishing Co., 1910.

Calendar of Delaware Wills, New Castle County, 1682-1800 (Images online)

http://www.ancestry.com/rd/prodredir.asp?sourceid=831&key=D6282

This database is a compilation of wills from New Castle County, Delaware, from 1682-1800. The records were abstracted and compiled by the Historical Research Committee of the Colonial Dames of Delaware. The wills include information on names, dates, places, relationships, and other important clues for family history research.

In preparing these wills, the Colonial Dames of Delaware research committee worked on the original wills as far as they existed in the Register's office and in the original Record of Probate, where the wills were missing. According to the committee, "Abstracts have been made of many wills, which, because of technical irregularities, were not probated, and consequently are not matters of record. The genealogical data thus presented gives the volume a unique advantage.

"For a period of years, in the early life of this Colony the law did not require that the probated wills filed in the Register's office should be recorded. Because of this, genealogists, and others interested in research work, were permitted to use the original wills, with the natural result that many were carried away, and many others suffered destruction or defacement from constant and careless handling."

Source Information: Ancestry.com. "Calendar of Delaware Wills, New Castle County, 1682-1800" [database online]. Provo, UT: Ancestry.com, 2002. Original data: "A Calendar of Delaware Wills New Castle County 1682-1800." New York, NY: Frederick H. Hitchcock, 1911.

❧

California State Roster, 1909 Government and Military Records
http://www.ancestry.com/rd/prodredir.asp?sourceid=831&key=D6290

The information in this database was compiled from the book, *California Blue Book, or State Roster, 1909,* compiled by Charles Forrest Curry, Secretary of State, and Printed at the State Printing office, Sacramento, (no date given). This book contains a listing of more than 14,000 state and municipal employees of the State of California for the year 1909. The listing includes employees of various state institutions and municipal governments down to the city levels. Employees are given for most state institutions, such as hospitals, universities, prisons; fish and game wardens are even listed. This is an excellent source of location of families at the time of the 1910 Federal Census.

This book was indexed by Debra Graden, Leavenworth, Kansas. Copies of the page including the entry (and photos, if included) are available by sending $2 and a SASE (self-addressed stamped envelope) to:

Debra Graden
P. O. Box 281
Leavenworth, KS 66048-0281

Source Information: Graden, Debra, comp. "California State Roster, 1909 Government and Military records" [database online]. Provo, UT: Ancestry.com, 2002. Original data: *California Blue Book or State Roster, 1909.* State Printing Office, Sacramento CA, 1909.

❧

Casco Bay, Maine Directory, 1923-24 (Images online)
http://www.ancestry.com/rd/prodredir.asp?sourceid=831&key=D6283

This database contains the 1923-24 city directories for the Casco Bay, including the townships of Bailey, Bates, Bear, Birch, Bombazine, Brunswick Shore, Bustin's, Clapboard, Cliff, Cousins,

Cushing, Dingley's, Eagle, Great Chebeague, Great Diamond, Goose, Harpswell, Haskell, Hope, Jewells, Little Birch, Little Bustin's, Little Chebeaugue, Little Diamond, Little Whaleboat, Littlejohn's, Long, Mere Point, Orr's, Peaks, Pole, Pumpkin Knob, Ragged, Sebascodegan, Stave, and Whaleboat located in Cumberland County, Maine. In addition to providing the names of the heads of households, it provides their addresses and occupational information. A list of yachts and members of the Portland and Bay Yacht clubs. Also included are a business directory, information on local schools, churches, banks, societies, and other miscellaneous matter. Images of the original directory accompany this database.

Source Information: Ancestry.com. "Casco Bay, Maine Directory, 1923-24" [database online]. Provo, UT: Ancestry.com, 2002. Original data: "The Casco Bay Directory, 1923-24." Portland, ME: Crowley & Lunt, 1923.

🎔

Darien, Noroton, Noroton Heights, and New Canaan, Connecticut City Directory, 1958 (Images online)
http://www.ancestry.com/rd/prodredir.asp?sourceid=831&key=D6289

This database contains the 1958 city directory for the cities of Darien, New Canaan, Noroton, and Noroton Heights, and is located in Fairfield County, Connecticut. This directory combines six distinct directories: Alphabetical, Buyers, Classified, Governmental, Numerical, and Numerical Telephone Directory. In addition to providing the names of the heads of households, it provides their addresses and occupational information. Additional information included on local sales and services, churches, banks, societies, and other miscellaneous information.

Source Information: Ancestry.com. "Darien, Noroton, Noroton Heights, and New Canaan, Connecticut City Directory, 1958" [database online]. Provo, UT: Ancestry.com, 2002. Original data: "Darien, New Canaan Directory 1958, Noroton, and Noroton Heights." New Haven, CT: The Price & Lee Co., 1958.

❀

Dover Suburban, New Hampshire City Directory, 1936-37
http://www.ancestry.com/rd/prodredir.asp?sourceid=831&key=D6278

This database contains the 1936-37 city directory for Dover Suburban, including the cities of Barrington, Lee, Madbury, Newington, Salmon Falls, and Rollinsford located in Strafford County, New Hampshire. In addition to providing the names of the heads of households, it provides their addresses and occupational information. Also included are a business and street directory, information on local schools, churches, banks, societies, and other miscellaneous information.

Source Information: Ancestry.com. "Dover Suburban, New Hampshire City Directory, 1936-37" [database online]. Provo, UT: Ancestry.com, 2002. Original data: "The Dover Suburban New Hampshire Directory for Barrington, Lee, Madbury, Newington, Salmon Falls, Rollinsford, N.H., 1936-37, Volume 4." New Hampshire: W.E. Shaw, Publisher, 1936.

❀

Early Settlers of Alabama
http://www.ancestry.com/rd/prodredir.asp?sourceid=831&key=D6257

Alabama Territory was created on 3 March 1817 and officially became a state on 14 December 1819. This database gives historical and genealogical information about early settlers of the state of Alabama as recorded by Col. James Saunders. Saunders began to write a series of letters in April 1880, focusing on the early settlers of Lawrence County, Alabama, and the Tennessee Valley. Soon his work branched out to other areas and even some adjoining states. The letters began in 1880 and discontinued in 1889. Researchers can expect to find valuable historical information and personal insight about the people of Alabama through Col. Saunders' letters.

Source Information: Ancestry.com. "Early Settlers of Alabama" [database online] Provo, UT: Ancestry.com, 2002. Original data: Saunders, James Edmonds, Col. "Early Settlers of Alabama." New Orleans, LA: L. Graham & Son, printers, 1899.

Eliot and York, Main City Directory, 1923 (Images online)
http://www.ancestry.com/rd/prodredir.asp?sourceid=831&key=D6287

This database contains the 1923 city directory for the cities of Eliot and York located in York County, Maine. In addition to providing the names of the heads of households, it provides their addresses and occupational information. Images of the directory accompany this database.

Source Information: Ancestry.com. "Eliot and York, Maine City Directory, 1923" [database online]. Provo, UT: Ancestry.com, 2002. Original data: "The Eliot and York (York Harbor and York Beach) Maine Directory, 1923: Embracing a General Directory of the Inhabitants." Maine: W.E. Shaw, 1923.

Exeter, New Market, and South New Market, New Hampshire, 1872 (Images online)
http://www.ancestry.com/rd/prodredir.asp?sourceid=831&key=D6296

This database contains the 1872 city directory for the cities of Exeter, New Market, and South New Market located in Rockingham County, New Hampshire. In addition to providing the names of the heads of households, it provides their addresses and occupational information. Also included are a business and street directory, information on churches, banks, societies, origins and sketches of families, a register of deaths since 1840 and other miscellaneous information. Databases of the directory accompany this database.

Source Information: Ancestry.com. "Exeter, New Market, and South New Market, New Hampshire, 1872" [database online]. Provo, UT: Ancestry.com, 2002. Original data: "The Exeter, New Market and South New Market

Directory and History, 1872: Containing the Names of Residents of Each Town, Arranged Alphabetically; Business Directories, Town Registers, etc." Boston, MA: Dean Dudley, 1872.

🌸

First Settlers of Connecticut and Massachusetts: Genealogical Notes and Contributions

http://www.ancestry.com/rd/prodredir.asp?sourceid=831&key=D6261

This database is a collection of genealogical notes collected by Nathaniel Goodwin from the time of his appointment to the office of probate judge for Hartford, Connecticut, in 1833 and continued until late in his life. Mr. Goodwin was well known for his love of genealogy. He was an original incorporator of the Connecticut Historical Society and also vice president of the New England Historic Genealogical Society at the time of his passing. These notes are not designed to be complete genealogies. The collection gives names, dates, and other valuable information for some of the first settlers of Connecticut and Massachusetts.

Source Information: Ancestry.com. "First Settlers of Connecticut and Massachusetts: Genealogical Notes and Contributions" [database online]. Provo, UT: Ancestry.com, 2002. Original data: Goodwin, Nathaniel. "Genealogical Notes, or Contributions to the Family History of Some of the First Settlers of Connecticut and Massachusetts." New Orleans, LA: L. Graham & Son, printers, 1899.

🌸

Historical and Genealogical Miscellany: New York and New Jersey, Vol. I and II (Update adding Volume II)

http://www.ancestry.com/rd/prodredir.asp?sourceid=831&key=D6248
This database contains records for Volumes I and II in a series of five volumes containing historical and genealogical miscellany compiled by John Stillwell. These records were gathered together in an effort to record the Stillwell families in New York and New Jersey.

However, when Mr. Stillwell realized the value of preserving the records for others, the scope was broadened to include all records that he was searching. These volumes contain records of town court, early road surveys, cattle marks, and other miscellaneous matter for Richmond County, New York. There are also many church and court records from New Jersey.

Information included in Volume II:
- Court Records, Burlington, New Jersey
- Parish Register of St. Mary's (St. Ann's), Burlington, N.J.
- Inscriptions, St. Mary's Churchyard, Burlington, N.J.
- First Town Book of Middletown, N.J.
- Record of Ear Marks of Middletown, N.J.
- Record of the Baptist Church, Middletown, N.J.
- James Mott's Journal
- Inscriptions, Burying Grounds, Monmouth County, N.J.
- Bible Records, Monmouth County, N.J.
- Patents for Lands on Quit Rents, Monmouth County, N.J.
- Surveys of Lands on Quit Rents, Monmouth County, N.J.
- Warrants for Survey on Lands on Quit Rents, Monmouth County, N.J.
- Quit Rents of Shrewsbury, East New Jersey
- Quit Rents of Middletown, East New Jersey
- Gawen Lawrie's Accounts, East Jersey Quit Rents
- Account of Shrewsbury Patents
- Middletown Quit Rents
- Abstracts from Men's Monthly Meetings, Shrewsbury, N.J.

Source Information: Ancestry.com. "Historical and Genealogical Miscellany: New York and New Jersey, Vol. I and II" [database online]. Provo, UT: Ancestry.com, 2002. Original data: Stillwell, John E. "Historical and Genealogical Miscellany: Data Relating to the Settlement and Settlers of New York and New Jersey, Vol. I-V. New York, NY: [s.n.], 1903.

Historical and Genealogical Miscellany: New York and New Jersey Vols. I, II, and III (Update adding Volume III)
http://www.ancestry.com/rd/prodredir.asp?sourceid=831&key=D6248

This database contains records for Volumes I, II, and III in a series of five volumes containing historical and genealogical miscellany compiled by John Stillwell. These records were gathered together in an effort to record the Stillwell families in New York and New Jersey. However, when Mr. Stillwell realized the value of preserving the records for others, the scope was broadened to include all the records that he was searching. These volumes contain records of town court, early road surveys, cattle marks, and other miscellaneous matter for Richmond County, New York. There are also many church and court records from New Jersey.

Information included in Volume III:
- Applegate of Ocean County
- Applegates in Revolutionary War
- Applegate, Ashton, Bowne, Brown, Burrowes, Campbell, Chamberlain,Coward, Cox, Crawford, Dorset, Eaton, Edwards, Grover, Hartsborne,Holmes, Kearny, Lawrence, Leeds, Lippit and Lyell of Monmouth County
- Angell-Ashton—Bray of New Jersey
- Bray if Kinderhook
- Bray of Yarmouth, Massachusetts
- Curtis of Burlington and Monmouth Counties
- Fitz Randolph of New Jersey
- Jonathan Holmes' Diary
- Huet or Huit of New Jersey
- Leaming of Cape May County
- Leaming Diaries
- Triumphant Christian

Source Information: Ancestry.com. "Historical and Genealogical Miscellany: New York and New Jersey, Vol. I and II" [database online]. Provo, UT: Ancestry.com, 2002. Original data: Stillwell, John E. "Historical and Genealogical Miscellany:

Data Relating to the Settlement and Settlers of New York and New Jersey, Vol. I-V." New York, NY: [s.n.], 1903.

Historical and Genealogical Miscellany: New York and New Jersey, Vols I-IV (Update adding Volume IV)
http://www.ancestry.com/rd/prodredir.asp?sourceid=831&key=D6248

This database contains records for Volumes I, II, III, and IV of the series of five volumes containing historical and genealogical miscellany compiled by John Stillwell. These records were gathered together in an effort to record the Stillwell families in New York and New Jersey. However, when Mr. Stillwell realized the value of preserving the records for others, the scope was broadened to include all the records that he was searching. These volumes contain records of town court, early road surveys, cattle marks, and other miscellaneous matter for Richmond County, New York. There are also many church and court records from New Jersey

Information included in Volume IV:
- Mott of New York and New Jersey
- Seabrook of South Carolina
- Seabrook of Edisto Island
- Seabrook of Maryland
- Spicer of New York and New Jersey
- Morford, Morris, Mount, Murphy, Ogborne, Potter, Salter, Seabrook, Shepherd, and Stout of Monmouth County
- Line of John Stout, Richard Stout, Probable Descendants of Richard Stout, Mary Stout (Bowne), James Stout, Alice Stout (Throckmorton), Peter Stout, Sarah Stout (Pike), Jonathan Stout, Benjamin Stout, and David Stout

Source Information: Ancestry.com. "Historical and Genealogical Miscellany: New York and New Jersey, Vol. I-IV" [database online]. Provo, UT: Ancestry.com, 2002. Original data: Stillwell, John E. "Historical and Genealogical Miscellany: Data Relating to the Settlement and Settlers of New York and New Jersey, Vol. I-V." New York, NY: [s.n.], 1903.

🐾

Historical and Genealogical Miscellany: New York and New Jersey Vols. I-V (Update)
http://www.ancestry.com/rd/prodredir.asp?sourceid=831&key=D6248

This database contains records for Volumes I-V in a series of five volumes containing historical and genealogical miscellany compiled by John Stillwell. These records were gathered together in an effort to record the Stillwell families in New York and New Jersey. However, when Mr. Stillwell realized the value of preserving the records for others, the scope was broadened to include all the records that he was searching. These volumes contain records of town court, early road surveys, cattle marks, and other miscellaneous matter for Richmond County, New York. There are also many church and court records from New Jersey.

File being added:
Information included in Volume V:

- Layton, Taylor, Throckmorton,Wall, Walling, Watson, Whitlock,Winter and Woolley of Monmouth County, N.J.
- Tallman of New Jersey
- Tilton of New Jersey
- Tilton, unconnected lines
- Tilton, Miscellaneous
- White of New Jersey
- Woodward of New Jersey

Source Information: Ancestry.com. "Historical and Genealogical Miscellany: New York and New Jersey, Vol. I-V" [database online]. Provo, UT: Ancestry.com, 2002. Original data: Stillwell, John E. "Historical and Genealogical Miscellany: Data Relating to the Settlement and Settlers of New York and New Jersey, Vol. I-V." New York, NY: [s.n.], 1903.

✦

History of Waterford, Oxford County, Maine (Images online)
http://www.ancestry.com/rd/prodredir.asp?sourceid=831&key=D6288

Waterford is located in Oxford County, Maine. This database is a history of the town from its earliest beginnings to its centennial celebration in 1875. Information included are a history of the grant and survey of Waterford, 1690-1775; a plantation history of Waterford, 1775-97; a town history from 1797-1820 (before separation); a town history from 1820-75 (after separation); a record of families, centennial proceedings, and 1875; and a memorial of Reverend John A. Douglass.

The book came as a result of the Waterford Centennial Celebration of 1 September 1875. The records of families recorded in the volume were an afterthought to the centennial committee. The records may not be complete representations of Waterford families; however, they should yield very valuable clues for family history research in Waterford and the surrounding areas.

Source Information: Ancestry.com. "Waterford, Oxford County, Maine History" [database online]. Provo, UT: Ancestry.com, 2002. Original data: "The History of Waterford, Oxford County, Maine, Comprising Historical Address by Henry P. Warren; Record of Families, By Rev. William Warren, D.D.; Centennial Proceedings By Samuel Warren, Esq." Portland, ME: Hoyt, Fogg & Donham, 1879.

✦

Irish Settlers in North America Before 1850 (Images online)
http://www.ancestry.com/rd/prodredir.asp?sourceid=831&key=D6297

Reportedly, the first Irish settlers to North America came in the late 1600s. This database is a history of these Irish immigrants from these early times up until the United States Census in 1850. Thomas McGee paints an interesting picture of Irish settlements, churches, and influence in government. This volume is sure to prove useful in understanding the history of early Irish immigrants to North America.

Source Information: Ancestry.com. "Irish Settlers in North America before 1850" [database online]. Provo, UT: Ancestry.com, 2002. Original data: McGee, Thomas D'Arcy. "A History of the Irish Settlers in North America, From the Earliest Period to the Census of 1850." Boston, MA: Patrick Donahoe, 1852.

Jasper County, Iowa 1892 Farmers Directory
http://www.ancestry.com/rd/prodredir.asp?sourceid=831&key=D6266

This database is a transcription of the Jasper County "chapter" of the Farmers of Iowa directory, originally published in 1892. Jasper County is in central Iowa, just east of Polk County, home of the state capital of Des Moines. The county seat is in Newton. The original record provides the surname and given name or initials of farmers living in each county of Iowa, as well as the names of certain unspecified businesses (e.g., Rogers & Sons). At the end of the chapter, there is a separate section for farmers who live in Jasper County, but receive their mail at a post office in an adjoining county and/or state. There is no information from the publisher as to the completeness of the directory, or how it was prepared, although there is evidence that it was compiled from land ownership records. (A husband and wife in the compiler's genealogy [John T. Leach and Mrs. Amanda V. Leach] are listed separately [he in Prairie City, she in Newton] although they are known to have lived together in Prairie City for their entire marriage. Based on a contemporaneous plat map, Amanda Leach appears as the primary owner of the Newton property.)

It should be noted that the names have been transcribed exactly as printed. Common abbreviations were often used in the directory for some names with or without periods (e.g., Geo. for George, Wm. for William, Jas. for James), and they have been reproduced in that manner here. Certain compound or multiple surnames such as Van Dyke had a space between the two names, but others did not (VanDovinick). (Names beginning with "Mc" did not include a space after the "c"). Several names appear to have typographical errors, which have also been reproduced as printed.

A researcher using this database is advised to search variant forms of a surname, or to search part of a surname, if an expected name is not found.

Source Information: Olson, Larry, comp. "Jasper County, Iowa 1892 Farmers Directory" [database online]. Provo, UT: Ancestry.com, 2002. Original data: "Farmers of Iowa: a list of farmers of each county with postoffice [sic], 1892," Jasper County, Iowa, 1892. LDS microfilm 1024846, item 4.

This database is also included in the 1890 Census Reconstruction Project and can be searched through its main page at <http://www.ancestry.com/search/rectype/census/1890sub/main.htm>.

Leavenworth County, Kansas, Marriage Records, 1900-20
http://www.ancestry.com/rd/prodredir.asp?sourceid=831&key=D6267

In the late 1980s, The Church of Jesus Christ of Latter-day Saints (The LDS Church) microfilmed the record books at the Leavenworth County Courthouse. The marriage records for 1900 through 1920 are located on the Family History Library microfilm (FHL # 185431, 185768, 185769, 185770 and 185771), which are numbered 104 through 110 in the collections of the Leavenworth County Genealogical Society. The original marriage books were removed from the Leavenworth County Courthouse in 2000 and moved to the Leavenworth County Justice Center and are not readily available. The index of these records was compiled by Debra Graden. Copies of the marriage license may be obtained by sending $5 and a self-addressed stamped envelope to Debra Graden, P. O. Box 281, Leavenworth, Kansas 66048-0281.

Source Information: Graden, Debra. "Leavenworth County, Kansas, Marriage Records, 1900-1920" [database online]. Orem, UT: Ancestry, Inc., 2002.Original data: Leavenworth County Clerk. "Leavenworth County Marriages, 1900-20." Leavenworth County, KS, 1900-20.

❀

Manhattan New York City Directory: 1829-30 (Update adding G-Ho)
http://www.ancestry.com/rd/prodredir.asp?sourceid=831&key=D6259

The 1829 Longworth's New York City Directory lists those people residing or working in that year on the island of Manhattan who were interviewed. This database indexes persons with the last names A-Ho. In addition to the names of residents, business and professional people and companies, the directory mentions related occupations, home, and secondary addresses (sometimes including addresses in suburbs, such as Brooklyn and New Jersey). The population of the island of Manhattan in 1830 was approximately 197,115. This directory, published annually in the 1800s is an excellent source of genealogical and social data on early New York City and can be used to supplement the 1830 U.S. Census, which does not provide full names, addresses, or occupations. Additionally, one can analyze neighborhoods and determine who was living and working near an ancestor by viewing the data by individual streets.

This update adds: Surnames G-Ho

Source Information: Hollister, Catherine, comp. "Manhattan New York City Directory: 1829-30" [database online]. Provo, UT: Ancestry.com, 2002. Original data: "Longworth's American Almanac, New-York Register and City Directory for 1829." Published by Thomas Longworth, 15 Pine Street, New York, N.Y., 1829.

❀

Manhattan New York City Directory: 1829-30 (Update adding Ho-Ki)
http://www.ancestry.com/rd/prodredir.asp?sourceid=831&key=D6259

The 1829 Longworth's New York City Directory lists those people residing or working in that year on the island of Manhattan who were interviewed. This release indexes persons with the last names

A-Ki. In addition to the names of residents, business and professional people and companies, the directory mentions related occupations, home, and secondary addresses (sometimes including addresses in suburbs, such as Brooklyn and New Jersey). The population of Manhattan Island in1830 was approximately 197,115. This directory, published annually in the 1800s is an excellent source of genealogical and social data on early New York City and can be used to supplement the 1830 U.S. Census, which does not provide full names, addresses, or occupations. Additionally, one can analyze neighborhoods and determine who was living and working near an ancestor by viewing the data by individual streets.

File being added: Surnames Ho-Ki

Source Information: Hollister, Catherine, comp. "Manhattan New York City Directory: 1829-30. [database online] Provo, UT: Ancestry.com, 2002. Original data: "Longworth's American Almanac, New-York Register and City Directory for 1829." Published by Thomas Longworth, 15 Pine Street, New York, N.Y., 1829.

❧

New Bedford and Fairhaven, Massachusetts, City Directory, 1898 (Images Online)
http://www.ancestry.com/rd/prodredir.asp?sourceid=831&key=D6263

This database contains the 1898 city directory for the cities of New Bedford and Fairhaven, located in Bristol County, Massachusetts. In addition to providing the names of the heads of households, it provides their addresses and occupational information. Also included are a business and street directory, information on local schools, churches, banks, societies, and other miscellaneous information. Images of the original directory accompany this database.

Source Information: Ancestry.com. "New Bedford and Fairhaven, Massachusetts City Directory, 1898" [database online]. Provo, UT: Ancestry.com, 2002. Original data: "1898: New Bedford and Fairhaven Directory of the Inhabitants Institutions, Manufacturing Establishments, Societies, Business, Business Firms, Map, State Census, Etc." Boston, MA: W.A. Greenough & Company, 1898.

※

New Haven, Connecticut City Directory, 1860-61 (Images online)
http://www.ancestry.com/rd/prodredir.asp?sourceid=831&key=D6256

This database contains the 1860-61 city directory for the city of New Haven, located in New Haven County, Connecticut. In addition to providing the names of the heads of households, it provides their addresses and occupational information. Also included are a business directory, information on local schools, churches, banks, societies, and other miscellaneous matter. Images of the original directory accompany this database.

Source Information: Ancestry.com. "New Haven, Connecticut City Directory, 1860-61" [database online]. Provo, UT: Ancestry.com, 2002. Original data: "Price and Lee's New Haven City Directory, 1860-61." New Haven, CT: Price & Lee Company, 1860-61.

※

New London, Connecticut City Directory, 1859-60 (Images online)
http://www.ancestry.com/rd/prodredir.asp?sourceid=831&key=D6265

This database contains the 1859-60 city directory for the city of New London, located in New London County, Connecticut. In addition to providing the names of the heads of households, it provides their addresses and occupational information. Also included are a business directory, information on local schools, churches, banks, societies, and other miscellaneous matter. Images of the original directory accompany this database.

Source Information: Ancestry.com. "New London, Connecticut City Directory, 1859-60" [database online]. Provo, UT: Ancestry.com, 2002. Original data: "New London Directory, 1859-60." New Haven, CT: Price & Lee Company, 1859-60.

❧

New York Births and Baptisms: Schoharie and Mohawk Valleys
http://www.ancestry.com/rd/prodredir.asp?sourceid=831&key=D6292

First settled by the Dutch in the seventeenth century and later acquired by the British, New York is one of the most important states in the history of the United States. This collection of birth and baptism records, compiled by Arthur and Nancy Kelly, was taken from the New York church registers and minister's records 1694-1906, and town birth records 1846-1849. It contains over 56,000 records from Fulton, Herkimer, Montgomery, Schenectady, and Saratoga Counties and provides details on more than 225,000 individuals. In addition to the child's name and date of birth or baptism, researchers may find information on parents' names, names of sponsors, and notes included in these vital records. Further information and books from which theses records were taken may be obtained from:

Arthur and Nancy Kelly
305 Cedar Heights Road
Rhinebeck, NY 12572

Church records provide the best substitute in New York State for vital record information. In particular, the Reformed and Lutheran churches kept excellent records, having the children baptized soon after their birth. Arthur Kelly has spent over 30 years transcribing and collecting early records of this area in an attempt to provide vital record information for the eighteenth and nineteenth centuries before civil records were required.

The following databases are included in this first release:
- Glenville Reformed Church, vital records, 1814-1914, Glenville, Schenectady
- First Reformed Church of Schenectady in the city of Schenectady, 1811-1852, Schenectady City, Schenectady—

Schenectady Reformed Church, Baptisms, 1694-1811, Schenectady City, Schenectady

- Niskayuna Reformed Church, 1783-1860, Niskayuna, Schenectady
- Births recorded by Mrs. Mary Stevens, midwife of Schenectady, NY, 1767-1788, Schenectady City, Schenectady—Christ Episcopal Church, Duanesburgh, 1766-1882, Duanesburgh, Schenectady
- Records of the First Reformed Church of Scotia, New York, 1818-1899, Glenville, Schenectady

Source Information: Ancestry.com. "New York Births and Baptisms, Schoharie and Mohawk Valleys" [database online]. Provo, UT: Ancestry.com, 2002. Original data: Arthur, Kelly, and Nancy. Original data extracted by Arthur and Nancy Kelly of Kinship Publishers from various church registers in Fulton, Herkimer, Montgomery, Schenectady, and Saratoga Counties in New York.

***

Notes of Livermore, in Androscoggin County, Maine (Formerly in Oxford County, Maine)
http://www.ancestry.com/rd/prodredir.asp?sourceid=831&key=D6274

This database contains historical, descriptive, and personal notes for Livermore in Androscoggin, which was formerly in Oxford County, Maine. It was compiled by Israel Washburn. These records also contain a history of Livermore and the area. In addition, the work provides a variety of valuable information including names and dates of important events in the lives of the people of Livermore.

Source Information: Ancestry.com. "Notes of Livermore, in Androscoggin (formerly in Oxford) County, Maine" [database online]. Provo, UT: Ancestry.com, 2002. Original data: Washburn, Israel. "Notes; Historical, Descriptive, and Personal, of Livermore, in Androscoggin (formerly in Oxford) County, Maine." Portland, ME: B. Thurston & Co., 1874.

Pepperell, Dunstable, Shirley & Townsend, Massachusetts City Directory, 1907-08 (Images online)

http://www.ancestry.com/rd/prodredir.asp?sourceid=831&key=D6270

This database contains the 1907-1908 city directory for the cities of Pepperell, Dunstable, Shirley and Townsend, located in Middlesex County, Massachusetts. In addition to providing the names of the heads of households, it provides their addresses and occupational information. Also included are a business and street directory, information on local schools, churches, banks, societies, and other miscellaneous information. Images of the original directory accompany this database.

Source Information: Ancestry.com. "Pepperell, Dunstable, Shirley & Townsend, Massachusetts, City Directory, 1907-08" [database online]. Provo, UT: Ancestry.com, 2002. Original data: "Pepperell, Dunstable, Shirley, Townsend Massachusetts Directory Containing Alphabetical Lists of the Residents, Churches, Schools, Societies, Town Officers, Etc., and Street and Business Directories, 1907-08." Boston, MA: Guy Richardson, Publisher, 1907-08.

Records of the Town of East Hampton, Long Island, Suffolk County, New York, Vol. 2, 4, and 5

http://www.ancestry.com/rd/prodredir.asp?sourceid=831&key=D6271

This database includes records from the town of East Hampton, Long Island in Suffolk County, New York for volumes 2, 4 and 5 in a series of six volumes. Volume 2 covers the time period of 1679-1702, volume 4 from 1734-1849 and volume 5 the years 1850-1900. The volumes contain various information including births, marriages, death, town history, Indian place names, and more.

Source Information: Ancestry.com. "Records of the Town of East-Hampton, Long Island, Suffolk County, New York, Vol. 2, 4, and 5" [database online]. Provo, UT: Ancestry.com, 2002. Original data: "Records of the Town of East Hampton, Long

Island, Suffolk Co., N.Y.: with other ancient documents of historic value East Hampton (N.Y.), Vol. 2, 4 and 5." Sag-Harbor, NY: J.H. Hunt, printer, 1887-1905.

🌺

Rockland and Abington, Massachusetts City Directory, 1904 (Images online)
http://www.ancestry.com/rd/prodredir.asp?sourceid=831&key=D6260

This database contains the 1904 city directory for the cities of Rockland and Abington, located in Plymouth County, Massachusetts. In addition to providing the names of the heads of households, it provides their addresses and occupational information. Also included are a business and street directory, information on local schools, churches, banks, societies, and other miscellaneous information. This database is also linked to images of the original directory.

Source Information: Ancestry.com. "Rockland and Abington, Massachusetts City Directory, 1904" [database online]. Provo, UT: Ancestry.com, 2002. Original data: "Resident and Business Directory of Rockland and Abington, Massachusetts, 1904: containing a complete resident, street and business directory, town officers, schools, societies, churches, post-offices, rates of postage, incorporation and population of all towns in Massachusetts the census of 1840 and 1900." Hopkinton, MA: A.E. Foss & Company, 1904.

🌺

Rockland and Hanover, Massachusetts City Directory, 1898 (Images online)
http://www.ancestry.com/rd/prodredir.asp?sourceid=831&key=D6272

This database contains the 1898 city directory for the cities of Rockland and Hanover, located in Plymouth County, Massachusetts. In addition to providing the names of the heads of households, it provides their addresses and occupational information. Also included are a business and street directory, information on local schools, churches, banks, societies, and other miscellaneous information.

Source Information: Ancestry.com. "Rockland and Hanover, Massachusetts City

Directory, 1898" [database online]. Provo, UT: Ancestry.com, 2002. Original data: "Resident and Business Directory of Rockland and Hanover, Massachusetts, for 1898." Needham, MA: A.E. Foss & Co., 1898.

❀

Salem, Canobie Lake District, Pelham, and Atkinson, New Hampshire City Directory, 1912 (Images online)
http://www.ancestry.com/rd/prodredir.asp?sourceid=831&key=D6281

This database contains the 1912 city directory for the cities of Salem, Canobie Lake District, Pelham, and Atkinson located in Rockingham County, New Hampshire. In addition to providing the names of the heads of households, it provides their addresses and occupational information. Also included are a business and street directory, information on local schools, churches, banks, societies, and other miscellaneous information.

Source Information: Ancestry.com. "Salem, Canobie Lake District, Pelham, and Atkinson, New Hampshire City Directory, 1912" [database online]. Provo, UT: Ancestry.com, 2002. Original data: "The Salem, Canobie Lake District, Pelham and Atkinson New Hampshire Directory 1912: Embracing a General Directory of the Inhabitants, Classified Business and Miscellaneous Directory, Streets, Roads, Postoffice and Localities of Each Town." Boston, MA: W.E. Shaw, 1912.

❀

Scotch-Irish: The Scot in North Britain, North Ireland, and North America, Vol. 2
http://www.ancestry.com/rd/prodredir.asp?sourceid=831&key=D6264

This database contains a large variety of information related to the Scotch-Irish, but focuses on many of the early Scotch-Irish families in colonial America. Chapter topics include the emigration and settlement of Scotch-Irish, common Scottish names, Scottish martyrs, Scots in Ireland, and some genealogical notes. While largely historical in nature there is much valuable genealogical data throughout.

Source Information: Ancestry.com. "Scotch-Irish: The Scot in North Britain, North

119

Ireland and North America" [database online]. Provo, UT: Ancestry.com, 2002. Original data: Hanna, Charles A. "The Scotch-Irish or the Scot in North Britain, North Ireland and North America, Vol. 2." New York, NY: Putnam, 1902.

❧

Virginia County Records, Volume VI
http://www.ancestry.com/rd/prodredir.asp?sourceid=831&key=D6280

The records in this series were compiled as part of a series known as the "Virginia County Records" and were edited by William Armstrong Crozier. This database is Volume VI and was published in 1909. The volume includes wills, land grants, and marriage bonds as well as other miscellaneous information on early Virginia settlers.

The following information is included in this volume:
- Elizabeth City Wills
- Rappahannock County Wills
- York County Wills
- Hanover County Wills
- Early Settlers in Virginia
- Surry County Records
- Revolutionary Soldiers
- Isle of Wight County Land Grants
- Elizabeth City Land Grants
- Northumberland County Land Grants
- Westmoreland County Land Grants
- York County, Land Grants
- Henrico County Land Grants
- Lancaster County Land Grants
- Fauquier County Land Grants
- Accomac County Land Grants
- Northampton Marriage Bonds

Source Information: Ancestry.com. "Virginia County Records, Vol. VI" [database online]. Provo, UT: Ancestry.com, 2002. Original data: edit. Crozier, William Armstrong. "Virginia County Records, Volume VI." Hasbrouck Heights, NJ: The Genealogical Association, 1909.

❧

Virginia County Records: Westmoreland County, Volume I
http://www.ancestry.com/rd/prodredir.asp?sourceid=831&key=D6277

The records in this series were compiled as part of a series known as the "Virginia County Records" and were edited by William Armstrong Crozier. This database is Volume I in that series and includes wills, land grants, and militia records for the county of Westmoreland in Virginia.

Source Information: Ancestry.com. "Virginia County Records: Westmoreland County, Vol. I" [database online]. Provo, UT: Ancestry.com, 2002. Original data: edit. Crozier, William Armstrong. "Virginia County Records, New Series, Volume I, Westmoreland County." Hasbrouck Heights, NJ: The Genealogical Association, 1913.

❧

Virginia County Records, Volume VII
http://www.ancestry.com/rd/prodredir.asp?sourceid=831&key=D6286

The records in this series were compiled as part of a series known as the Virginia County Records and were edited by William Armstrong Crozier. This database is Volume VII and was published in 1909. The volume includes wills, land grants, and marriage bonds as well as other miscellaneous information on early Virginia settlers. The following information is included in this volume:

- Accomac (now Accomack) County Land Grants
- Henrico County Land Grants
- York County Land Grants
- Sussex County Land Grants
- Patrick County Land Grants
- Goochland County Land Grants
- Caroline County Land Grants

- Virginia Revolutionary Soldiers
- Northampton County Marriage Bonds
- Orange County Marriage Bonds
- Revolutionary Pensioners
- Early Settlers in Virginia
- Richmond County Wills
- Rappahannock County Wills
- Family History, Morton, Anderson, Lanier

Source Information: Ancestry.com. "Virginia County Records, Vol. VII" [database online]. Provo, UT: Ancestry.com, 2002. Original data: edit. Crozier, William Armstrong. "Virginia County Records, Volume VII." Hasbrouck Heights, NJ: The Genealogical Association, 1909.

❧

Virginia County Records, Volume IX
http://www.ancestry.com/rd/prodredir.asp?sourceid=831&key=D6293

The records in this series were compiled as part of a series known as the Virginia County Records and were edited by William Armstrong Crozier. This database is Volume IX and was published in 1911. The volume includes wills, land grants, and marriage bonds as well as other miscellaneous information on early Virginia settlers. The following information is included in this volume:

- Rappahannock County Land Grants
- Richmond County Land Grants
- Caroline County Marriage Bonds
- Early Settlers in Virginia
- Henrico County Records
- Loudoun County Militia Lists
- Virginia Revolutionary Soldiers
- Northampton County, Wills
- Lyon Family Records

Source Information: Ancestry.com. "Virginia County Records, Volume IX" [database online] Provo, UT: Ancestry.com, 2002. Original data: edit. Crozier, William Armstrong "Virginia County Records, Volume IX." Hasbrouck Heights, NJ: The Genealogical Association, 1911.

🎔

Watertown, Massachusetts Records of Births, Deaths, and Marriages, 1630-93 (Images online)

http://www.ancestry.com/rd/prodredir.asp?sourceid=831&key=D6298

Established in 1630, Watertown was one of the largest settlements of its time. Watertown lies in Middlesex County, Massachusetts, six miles from Boston. This database includes births, marriages, and deaths from Watertown for the years 1630-93. This book is a supplement to a larger collection. The records were transcribed and verified by Watertown clerk Fred E. Pritchett in 1894.

Source Information: Ancestry.com. "Watertown, Massachusetts Records of Births, Deaths, and Marriages, 1630-1693" [database online]. Provo, UT: Ancestry.com, 2002. Original data: "Watertown records: comprising the first and second books of town proceedings with the lands grants and possessions, also the proprietors' book and the first book and supplement of births and deaths and marriages Historical Society of Watertown (Mass.)." Watertown, MA: Fred G. Baker, 1894.

🎔

Wellesley, Massachusetts City Directory, 1907 (Images online)

http://www.ancestry.com/rd/prodredir.asp?sourceid=831&key=D6268

This database contains the 1907 city directory for the city of Wellesley, located in Norfolk County, Massachusetts. In addition to providing the names of the heads of households, it provides their addresses and occupational information. Also included are a business directory, information on local schools, churches, banks, societies, and other miscellaneous matter. Images of the original directory accompany this database.

Source Information: Ancestry.com. "Wellesley, Massachusetts City Directory, 1907" [database online]. Provo, UT: Ancestry.com, 2002. Original data: "The Wellesley Massachusetts Directory 1907 of the inhabitants, institutions, societies, manufacturing business firms, etc." Boston, MA: W.E. Shaw, Compiler and Publisher, 1907.

"One of the most admirable things about history is, that almost as a rule we get as much information out of what it does not say as we get out of what it does say. And so, one may truly and axiomatically aver this, to-wit: that history consists of two equal parts; one of these halves is statements of fact, the other half is inference, drawn from the facts. To the experienced student of history there are no difficulties about this; to him the half which is unwritten is as clearly and surely visible, by the help of scientific inference, as if it flashed and flamed in letters of fire before his eyes. When the practised eye of the simple peasant sees the half of a frog projecting above the water, he unerringly infers the half of the frog which he does not see. To the expert student in our great science, history is a frog; half of it is submerged, but he knows it is there, and he knows the shape of it."

— *Mark Twain, "The Secret History of Eddypus"*

May 2002
Census Images Online

Ancestry.com continues to update its Census Images Online Project, increasing the value of census subscriptions. The following databases are accessible only by Ancestry.com Census Collection subscribers.

1930 U.S. Census Images and Indexes

Over the past few weeks Ancestry.com has released images of the 1930 U.S. Federal Census for Missouri and an index for the District of Columbia. Images from the 1930 Census are now available for:

- California
- Connecticut
- Delaware (with every-name index!)
- District of Columbia (with every-name index!)
- Maine
- Massachusetts
- Missouri
- New Hampshire
- New Jersey
- Rhode Island
- Utah (with every-name index!)
- Vermont

(Every name indexes are being created for all states in this census year and will be posted as they become available.)

1920 U.S. Census Indexes

Images are currently available for all states. Ancestry.com now has indexed 95% of the 1920 census online:

- Alabama, 683,696 names (96%)
- Arizona, 131,965 names (100%)
- Arkansas, 580,364 names (100%)
- California, 1,478,508 names (99%)
- Colorado, 320,308 names (95%)
- Connecticut, 511,509 names (100%)
- Delaware, 82,045 names (100%)
- District of Columbia, 194,258 names (89%)
- Florida, 350,325 names (100%)
- Georgia, 904,077 names (100%)
- Idaho, 122,717 names, (89%)
- Illinois, 2,268,878 names (100%)
- Indiana, 1,009,238 names (100%)
- Iowa, 686,582 names (87%)
- Kansas, 596,992 names (97%)
- Kentucky, 732,681 names (100%)
- Louisiana, 587,435 names (97%)
- Maine, 264,001 names (93%)
- Maryland, 514,662 names (100%)
- Massachusetts, 1,418,206 names (100%)
- Michigan, 912,799 names (71%)
- Minnesota, 764,559 names (98%)
- Mississippi, 445,629 names (82%)
- Missouri, 1,177,369 names (100%)
- Montana, 207,211 names (100%)
- Nebraska, 382,802 names (92%)
- Nevada, 38,015 names (100%)
- New Hampshire, 172,318 names (100%)
- New Jersey, 1,150,870 names (100%)
- New Mexico, 143,455 names (100%)
- New York, 4,170,520 names (100%)
- North Carolina, 678,329 names (98%)
- North Dakota, 184,873 names (100%)

- Ohio, 2,053,314 names (100%)
- Oklahoma, 628,658 names (100%)
- Oregon, 281,433 names (100%)
- Pennsylvania, 3,121,914 names (100%)
- Rhode Island, 187,327 names (92%)
- South Dakota, 194,467 names (100%)
- Tennessee, 710,412 names (100%)
- Texas, 1,457,777 names (99%)
- Utah, 131,639 names (100%)
- Vermont, 129,687 names (100%)
- Virginia, 700,365 names (100%)
- Washington, 672,050 names (100%)
- West Virginia, 401,096 names (100%)
- Wisconsin, 891,260 names (100%)
- Wyoming, 41,464 names (60%)

For more information on everything that is available in Ancestry.com's Census Collection, go to:
http://www.ancestry.com/rd/census.htm

To subscribe to Ancestry.com's Images Online and/or Ancestry.com databases, go to:
http://www.ancestry.com/rd/redir.asp?sourceid=831&targetid=3506

Every Name Indexes
Every name indexes are being created for 1930 Census year and will be posted as they become available.

May 2002
UK/Ireland Databases

The following databases are accessible only by Ancestry.com UK/Ireland subscribers.

Burke's Commons of Great Britain and Ireland
http://www.ancestry.com/rd/prodredir.asp?sourceid=831&key=D6269

This database details information found in John Burke's history of landed gentry or commoners of Great Britain and Ireland, printed in 1837 and 1838 and includes information about those persons who owned land or held high official rank, but were not considered nobility. Biographies often contain information about names, places, dates of vital events such as birth, marriage and death, occupations, and occasionally, an achievement of a coat of arms.

Source Information: Ancestry.com. "Burke's Commoners of Great Britain and Ireland" [database online]. Provo, UT: Ancestry.com, 2002. Original data: "A genealogical and heraldic history of the landed gentry; or, Commoners of Great Britain and Ireland enjoying territorial possessions or high official rank: but uninvested with heritable honours." London: Colburn, 1837-38.

Cheshire, England: Parish and Probate Records (Update)
http://www.ancestry.com/rd/prodredir.asp?sourceid=831&key=D5856

This update adds:
- Lancashire & Cheshire: Miscellanies and an Index of Infra Wills
- Lancashire & Cheshire: Miscellanies containing:
  A list of clergy for, 1541-42; a list of the tenths and subsidy payable to the Archdeaconry of Chester
  Chorley survey
  List of the wills, inventories, administration bonds, and testamentary depositions, 1487-1620
  Preserved at the diocesan registry, Chester
  Lancashire & Cheshire: Cases in the Court of Star Chamber, 1499-1528
  Lancashire & Cheshire:—Calendar of parsons commemorated in Monumental inscriptions, Abstracts of Wills, and Administrations
  A list of the Freeholders in Cheshire, 1578
  The ordination Register of Chester, 1542-58
  List of the Wills, Inventories, etc., 1621-1700
  Preserved at the Diocesan Registry, Chester
  The Book of the Abbot of Combermere, 1289-1529
  Includes Rentals of Wych Malbanke
- Cheshire: Stockport—Probate Records, 1578-1619

Source Information: Ancestry.com. "Cheshire, England: Parish and Probate Records" [database online]. Provo, UT: Ancestry.com, 2001. Original data: Electronic databases created from various publications of parish and probate records.

※

Suffolk, England:Parish and Probate Records (Update)
http://www.ancestry.com/rd/prodredir.asp?sourceid=831&key=D5936

This update adds:
Suffolk: West Stow Parish Registers 1558-1850 and Wordwell Parish Registers, 1580-1850
- Monumental Inscriptions in West Stow Church

- Monumental Inscriptions in West Stow Churchyard
- Lay Subsidies for West Stow and Wordwell for the years 1327, 1341, 1539, 1543, 1544, 1549, 1550, 1566, 1576, 1581, 1598, 1599, 1620, 1625, 1627, 1639, 1640, 1641, 1675
- Rectors and Curates of West Stow
- Rectors and Curates of Wordwell
- Christian Names
- Wills
- Inquisition Post Mortem Edmundi Crofts, 1558
- Lost Tombstones
- Lucas Family
- Crofts Family
- Edward Proger
- The Proger Brothers
- The Fowke Family
- The Edwards Family
- Lessees of the Hall
- West Stow Hall
- The Sale
- Roman and Saxon Antiquities (A Roman Kiln, A Saxon Cemetery, Celtic Remains)
- The Owners of Wordwell
- Tenants of Wordwell Hall Farm
- Captain Booty Harvey

Source Information: Ancestry.com. "Suffolk, England: Parish and Probate Records" [database online]. Provo, UT: Ancestry.com, 2001. Original data: Electronic databases created from various publications of parish and probate records.

❁

Yorkshire, England: Parish and Probate Records (Update)
http://www.ancestry.com/rd/prodredir.asp?sourceid=831&key=D5982

This update adds:
- Yorkshire: Bradfield—Parish Registers (Christenings, Marriages & Burials): 1559-1722

- Yorkshire: Braithwell—Parish Registers
  (Christenings, Marriages & Burials), 1559-1774
  Baptisms: 1559-1772
  Marriages: 1559-1760
  Burials: 1559-1774
- Yorkshire: Braithwell—Parish Registers, 1754-1837
  Baptisms: 1767-1837
  Burials: 1767-1837
  Marriages: 1754-1837
- Yorkshire: Brandesburton—Parish Registers, 1558-1837
- Yorkshire: Brantingham—Parish Registers, 1653-1812
- Yorkshire: Brodsworth—Parish Registers, 1538-1813
- Yorkshire: Bubwith—Parish Registers, 1600-01, 1623-1767
- Yorkshire: Burghwallis—Parish Registers, 1596-1812
- Yorkshire: Burnsall—Parish Registers, 1813-1900
- Yorkshire: Burnsall—St. Mary's Chapel Registers, 1567-1812
- Yorkshire: Burton, Fleming—Parish Registers, 1538-1812
- Yorkshire: Calverley—Parish Registers, 1574-1649,
  Testamentary Burials: 1404, 1488, 1403, 1466, 1475, 1588,
  1616, 1628, 1625, 1500, 1524, 1548, 1563
  Churchwardens of Calverley
  Baptisms, 1574-1644
  Marriages, 1596-1649
  Burials, 1596-1644
  Calverley Burials & Marriages at Bradford
- Yorkshire: Calverley & Pudsey—Parish Registers, 1681-1720
  Notes From Wills Proved At York
  Calverley Wills
  Calverley Soke. Inhabitants Of Pudsey
  Pudsey Nonconformist Register
  Baptisms: 1710-17
  Vicars of Calverley

Source Information: Ancestry.com. "Yorkshire, England: Parish and Probate Records" [database online]. Provo, UT: Ancestry.com, 2001. Original data: Electronic databases created from various publications of parish and probate records.

The Gettysburg Address

Four score and seven years ago our fathers brought forth upon this continent, a new nation, conceived in liberty, and dedicated to the proposition that all men are created equal.

Now we are engaged in a great civil war, testing whether that nation, or any nation so conceived and so dedicated, can long endure. We are met on a great battlefield of that war. We have come to dedicate a portion of that field, as a final resting place for those who here gave their lives that this nation might live. It is altogether fitting and proper that we should do this.

But in a larger sense, we cannot dedicate, we cannot consecrate, we cannot hallow this ground. The brave men, living and dead, who struggled here, have consecrated it, far above our poor power to add or detract. The world will little note, nor long remember what we say here, but it can never forget what they did here. It is for us, the living, rather to be dedicated here to the unfinished work, which they who fought here have thus far so nobly advanced.

It is rather for us to be here dedicated to the great task remaining before us, that from these honored dead we take increased devotion to that cause for which they gave the last full measure of devotion; that we here highly resolve that these dead shall not have died in vain; that this nation, under God, shall have a new birth of freedom, and that this government of the people, by the people, and for the people shall not perish from this earth.

—Abraham Lincoln, 19 November 1863
http://www.loc.gov/exhibits/gadd/

More Memorial Day Speeches

Oliver Wendell Holmes, Jr. "The Soldier's Faith" (30 May 1884)
http://www.people.virginia.edu/~mmd5f/holmesfa.htm

Oliver Wendell Holmes, Jr. "In Our Youth Our Hearts Were Touched With Fire" (30 May 1895)
http://www.people.virginia.edu/~mmd5f/memorial.htm

May 2002
Historical Newspaper
Collection

The following databases are accessible only by Ancestry.com Historical Newspaper Collection subscribers.

NEWSPAPERS CAN BE USED TO FIND valuable genealogical information about historical events in the lives of our ancestors. They supply all sorts of clues about vital statistics (birth, marriage, and death announcements), obituaries, local news, biographical sketches, legal notices, immigration, migration, and shipping information and other historical items that place our ancestors in the context of the society in which they lived.

The ability to search the newspapers is dependent upon the quality of the original images. The images for this newspaper can be browsed sequentially, or via links to specific images, which may be obtained through the search results. Over time the name of a newspaper may have changed and the time span it covered may not always be consistent. The date range represented in this database is not necessarily the complete published set available. Check the local library or historical society in the area in which your ancestors lived for more information about other available newspapers.

✼

Fort Wayne News (Fort Wayne, Indiana)
http://www.ancestry.com/rd/prodredir.asp?sourceid=831&key=D6254

1895-97 (1,443 pages)
1898 (1,625 pages)
1899 (2,414 pages)
1900 (1,132 pages)
1901-02 (1,115 pages)
1903 (947 pages)
1904, 1907 (1,586 pages)
1909-10 (947 pages)
1911 (1,074 pages)
1912 (2,148 pages)
1913 (4,256 pages)

The Fort Wayne News was located in Fort Wayne, Indiana. This database is a fully searchable text version of the newspaper for the years 1895-97.

Source Information: Ancestry.com. "The Fort Wayne News" (Fort Wayne, Indiana) [database online]. Provo, UT: Ancestry.com, 2002. Original data: Database created from microfilm copies of the newspaper.

✼

"Fort Wayne Sentinel" (Fort Wayne, Indiana)
http://www.ancestry.com/rd/prodredir.asp?sourceid=831&key=D6178

1894-95 (1,488 pages)
1896-97 (1,389 pages)
1898-99 (2,296 pages)
1900 (1,230 pages)
1901 (1,194 pages)

1902 (1,174 pages)
1903; 1906-07 (1,654 pages)
1908-09; 1912 (2,113 pages)

The Fort Wayne Sentinel newspaper was located in Fort Wayne, Indiana. This database is a fully searchable text version of the newspaper for the years 1894-99, as well as 1905 and 1909 (2,296 pages).

Source Information: Ancestry.com. "Fort Wayne Sentinel (Fort Wayne, Indiana)" [database online]. Provo, UT: Ancestry.com, 2002. Original data: Database created from microfilm copies of the newspaper.

Nevada State Journal (Update adding newspapers from 1920 and 1922)
http://www.ancestry.com/rd/prodredir.asp?sourceid=831&key=D6182

The Nevada State Journal newspaper was located in Reno, Nevada. This database is a fully searchable text version of newspapers for the years 1870-75, 1911-13, 1916-18.

This update adds newspapers from 1920 and 1922 (1,528 pages)

Source Information: Ancestry.com. "Nevada State Journal" (Reno, Nevada) [database online]. Provo, UT: Ancestry.com, 2002. Original data: Database created from microfilm copies of the newspaper.

New York Times (Update adding 1905-06)
http://www.ancestry.com/rd/prodredir.asp?sourceid=831&key=D6231

The New York Times newspaper was located in New York, New York. This database is a fully searchable text version of the newspaper for the years 1881 to 1900 and 1905 to 1906.

This update adds 1905-06 (1,550 pages)

Source Information: Ancestry.com. "New York Times (New York, New York), 1881-1900; 1905-06" [database online]. Provo, UT: Ancestry.com, 2002. Original data: Database created from microfilm copies of the newspaper.

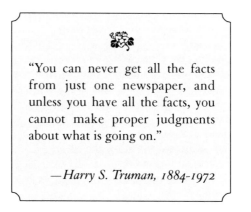

Reno Weekly Gazette and Stockman (Reno, Nevada), 1889; 1894-99
http://www.ancestry.com/rd/prodredir.asp?sourceid=831&key=D6262

The Reno Weekly Gazette and Stockman newspaper was located in Reno, Nevada. This database is a fully searchable text version of the newspaper for the years 1889 and 1894 to 1899 (1832 pages).

This is the first release of data for this title.

Source Information: Ancestry.com. "Reno Weekly Gazette and Stockman (Reno, Nevada)" [database online]. Provo, UT: Ancestry.com, 2002. Original data: Database created from microfilm copies of the newspaper.

> "You can never get all the facts from just one newspaper, and unless you have all the facts, you cannot make proper judgments about what is going on."
>
> *—Harry S. Truman, 1884-1972*

Clippings of the Day

From the "Weekly Evening Gazette" (Reno, Nevada), 16 Jan 1879, page 1

The Cleavland [sic] *Herald* thinks that if Sunday school books were not made so fearfully and drearily good, boys would not turn in despair to pernicious juvenile literature. Boys are chock full of human nature and they do not relish the drivelling, [sic] dreary goodness which uproots at once every bit of depravity in the heart, and takes from them all the rollicking tendencies of boyhood, leaving them as cold and unlikely to yield to temptation as the north side of a stone meeting house.

From "Dawson's Fort Wayne Daily Times," 14 May 1861, page 2
Local and Miscellaneous

• Frank Stinchcomb has returned, bringing Miss Minnie Shaw Stinchcomb, from Lancaster, O., to whom he was lately married. He is greeted by his friends for this new relation. It is a step in the best direction.

• Last night was enacted another of those scenes which may be properly called "a relic of barbarism." A gentleman had recently married, and returned to his parental home, and a set of rowdy young men and boys assembled there and most shamefully disgraced the town by their unnatural noise. The parent who allows his son to go into such a crowd, deserves the odium due to his rowdy child, which is punishment in the State prison; and yet there are those in this city who not only encourage their sons in it, but laugh at the disgrace it brings on the city.

A few years ago ex-Gov. Bebb of Ohio, then a resident of a country seat in Rockford county, Ill., was outraged on the occasion of the marriage of his son, by a set of rowdies who grew more and more insolent and vulgar as they were importuned to desist, until the Gov. at length unable to stand the insult, fired on the crowd, and sent the souls of some of the villains quickly to where they belonged, and wounded others. This timely and justifiable act put the balance to flight, and cured them and the rest of the rowdies of that region of the barbarous practice. The Gov. was indicted, tried and acquitted triumphantly, by a jury of the same county. An example ought to be made in Fort Wayne, and a score shot dead on the spot, that the city may be rid of their presence, and society saved their demoralizing influence.

Tis true older boys often seduce younger ones into such things, and often without the knowledge of honest parents; but then the parent who does not keep his son under such obedience as to know that he is not prowling around the streets at night, does his duty neither to society nor to his son.

We know not one of those engaged in that affair last night, and hence cannot tell what class they were from such knowledge, but their conduct convicts many, and they it is hoped may at once [curfew?] their habits.

From the "Nevada State Journal" 17 December 1870, page 1

A wag [joker] in Cincinnati bribed an unsophisticated band to play the Marseillaise [French National Anthem] in a beer garden in that city. A subscription is now being taken up to buy new instruments for the musicians, and the doctor's bill will be paid out of the Teutonic fund.

Why is a woodchuck like a sausage?
Because it's a ground hog.

From the "Fort Wayne Sentinel," 20 January 1909, page 1:
A corn shredder, of the species that has claimed so many arms and legs and is second only to the civil war in its output of dead and wounded, met its fate on the tracks of the Fort Wayne and Wabash Valley Traction company, near Roanoke, last November, according to a complaint filed in the circuit court today by Harry Coe, who seeks to recover $850 damages from the company.

Coe says that a crossing that afforded egress to the farm of Charles Nicodemus was allowed to become out of repair and that some boards that should have been there were absent when he attempted to pull his shredder across the tracks. It balked on him and in spite of the fact that he sent a flagman down the track to head off an interurban limited that was due about that time, did not prevent a collision in which the machine was demolished. He fixes its value at $650 and wants $200 more for attorney fees and costs. Wood & Aiken, of Wabash, filed the action.

From the "Nevada State Journal," 16 March 1872, page 3
Those Old Shanties
Those old shanties that stood in front of the business street, and were temporarily occupied as places of business after the fire, are mostly torn down. A few, however, yet remain and detract very much from the otherwise tasty appearance of our town. We should think there would be energy enough among our business men to pull them down.

"The beautiful Snow" still continues to fall on us in abundance. The "oldest inhabitant" predicts that we shall have the heaviest snow storm of the season in the month of March. As we have had one continued snow and rain storm of three weeks duration we hope the "oldest," as usual, is mistaken.

From the "Fort Wayne News," 4 June 1902, page 2
A Little Break Told
Stories of precocious youngsters seem to be in vogue just at present, so

it may be all right to revive the one of the little girl who had acquired in some mysterious way much to the distress of her mother, a line of words that are commonly classified as "swear words." The mother, like many another, thought perhaps the minister could accomplish what home training had failed to do and asked the clergyman who visited the house to exert his influence to cure the child of the distressing habit. Accordingly, while on a visit to the house, the minister took the child on his knee and explained to her all the dire consequences of using bad language, emphasizing the fact that no lady would do such a thing. When he felt that his work was taking effect, the child looked up and said: "Who told you I swore?" The preacher resorted to the bird fable and said smilingly, "O, a little bird whispered it." "Yes," said the little girl, "I bet it was one of them d—d sparrows."

From the "Fort Wayne News," 04 June 1902, page 6
Plucky Barnard Girls

How They Got In the Swim Despite Callow "Mere Men."

The lesson on the woman question recently administered to the young men students of Columbia university is strenuous enough to last them the rest of their lives if they are possessed of average masculine sense . . . The lesson is this: The world was made for woman also, and she herself, not callow college boys, is to decide where her place in it shall be.

From the very beginning the young men of that institution of learning which is the pride of New York city have persecuted the girls of Barnard college, the hall designed for young women students. The men's college paper has even gone so far in its sex insolence as to assert that Columbia is not a coed school at all. The university authorities, being men who belong to the twentieth century, are on the side of the women. When recently these authorities granted the Barnard girls for each Wednesday evening the use of the swimming pool of the university gymnasium, men students who enjoyed it all the rest of the time sent earthward and skyward a howl of foaming rage. They vowed by the Eternal, as it were, that they would rout the women out of that sacred he-tank or "bust." What was more, not even a female mosquito should buzz around the pie and doughnuts vended behind the college lunch counter.

"We men always have been victorious in the battle of the sexes, and we'll be again," they said.

The Barnard girls were troubled, but not dismayed.... Then the mills of the gods that at length crush into powder brutality, persecution and all wrong done by one party to another began to grind. They ground not "slowly" in this case, but quickly, the gods apparently deeming that her was an emergency requiring dispatch.

The story of the men's persecution of the women students was well ventilated in the newspapers, and the sympathies of reporter and editor were in every case on the side of the girls, which was a great help to them. After a few weeks the returns began to come in. Columbia boys looked down their noses, and an expression of glumness overspread their faces when one morning lately it was announced that an endowment of $500,000 had been secured for the enemy on whose neck they had sought to set their collective foot—the girls of Barnard.

Thus bad began, but worse remained behind. Less than a week after Barnard got its half million endowment once more the newspapers took up the tale and told how a generous anonymous benefactor of the feminine sex had given a quarter million more to build a magnificent gymnasium of their own for the Barnard girls, with a swimming pool especially that was to rival the baths of Diocletian in size and luxuriousness of equipment, a pool to which the boys' tank would be even as a washtub.

... But the crowning overthrow and rolling in the dust of the boys, the worstest worse, so to speak, is this: Adjacent to the college grounds is a plot which the Columbia Athletic club has been years trying to buy for an exercise field, and this now has actually been purchased under their noses for the young women of Barnard, where they may march, play ball and sprint at their own sweet will. Between the college campus whence the men tried so persistently to drive the women students altogether and the new athletic field there is to be a very high grillwork fence, through which the girls may bite their thumbs at the boys and say:

"You may go to grass with your old Wednesday tanking."

Yes, decidedly the Barnard college girls are in the swim.

[Note: This article was edited for length and the entire piece can be found, along with a drawing of "Barnard Girls in the Sacred He-Tank, Columbia University," at:

http://www.ancestry.com/rd/prodredir.asp?sourceid=831&key=D6254

Just click on "View Images of the Original Document," then 1902, June, 04, and skip to page 6.]

From the "Fort Wayne News," 4 June 1904, page 5
The Police Notes

Miss Mary Arnes, forelady at the Sixbey factory in this city, has returned from a visit at Bluffton. The News of that city says that Miss Arnes says she was hugged in the depot at Bluffton by the L. E. & W. operator Sunday night. Mr. Haney, the operator, denies the charge.

Adam Kalbach, of 1919 Force street, left his umbrella hanging on a stand in the market yesterday morning. Last night he telephoned the police and asked that a search be instituted for it. Forty men were out to work on the case.

From the "Nevada State Journal," 16 March 1872, page 2
A Savage or Fool

Some weeks since quite an excitement was made by the report of an attempted assassination of a student in the Catholic College at Fordham, New York. It is now said to have been a college boy's trick to frighten a student and have some fun. If so, it is only another illustration of the fact that there is a period in the life of boys when they act like savages or fools; even disgracing the Darwinian theory of descent.

This is the traveling age, and the sovereigns of the world, who in former times and until within a few years confined themselves chiefly to their own territories, have got fully into the spirit of seeing other lands. During the last twenty years, the sovereigns of Europe have been frequently exchanging visits. The Emperor of Brazil has just been making an extended tour of Europe, and we learn that the King of Siam is now traveling in India. These royal visits will do good to the kings and to their people, and it would do neither of them any harm if they would extend their journeys to this country. It might not make them Republicans, but it would give them some new ideas.

From the "Fort Wayne News," 5 April 1899, page 4

Chicago Voters yesterday did swat John P. Altgeld awful hard; but then, he needed it. Prof. Hall, who told the teachers in convention assembled here last week, that Nature is God, or words to that effect, has opened his mouth again at Chicago, with the result of proving that he is several kinds of an a--.

The telegrams announce that a great cheer went up from the crowds gathered on the outside, when the bridal pair appeared upon occasion of the Vanderbilt-Fair nuptials yesterday. There are just as many snobs in New York as anywhere.

From "The Fort Wayne News," 2 January 1896, page 3

Why Wear An Article of Dress That is Despised—Society Notes

Now that the new year has come, and all people are starting out anew to make the world more interesting, why cannot the woman who wishes to dress well and yet wear something satisfactory to herself, proclaim her ideas in regard to the despised bustle. For most women do despise it and are shrinking from the time when they will be compelled to wear it or be behind the times in fashion. Women rose up en masse against the introduction of the hoop skirt, and the unlucky article of dress disappeared from the earth. The same disposal of the bustle may be made if sensible women will practice what they preach in regard to the matter.

From the "Fort Wayne Journal Gazette," 10 December 1921

Hubby Wants Chance To Tell His Story

Whether the story of love turned to nothingness, of kicks and cuffs from the man who had sworn to cherish and protect her, told with tremulous lips by Mabel Hentzler to Judge Ballou yesterday morning in superior court has another side may yet be revealed in court.

Henry Hentzler, the husband, through his attorney, H. Waveland Kerr, yesterday afternoon filed a motion to set aside the divorce judgment taken by default and the motion will be argued tomorrow by Attorney Kerr and Attorney Carrie C. Warrington. So many people asked Mrs. Warrington to let them know when she was going to make her speech that she laughingly said she was going to publish an ad in the newspapers telling the time. In her testimony before Judge Ballou, Mrs. Hentzler said her husband told her:

"The sooner you go to a tuberculosis camp the sooner I shall be free."

This was his reply, she said, when she asked him to work in order that she might have medical attention for the lung trouble.

From the "Fort Wayne Journal Gazette," 10 December 1921
Legally Sane Now
Legally insane and didn't know it.

That was the condition in which George Angermaier (or Angermaker or Angermaler), Catholic priest, found himself recently, according to the testimony before Judge Ballou in superior court, when he was granted a writ of habeas corpus to free himself from the legal custody of Kent Sweet, county clerk.

About two years ago Father Angermaier had an illness during which his mind was temporarily affected. He was examined by a committee composed of Dr. Alfred L. Kane, Charles J. Rothschild, Edward J. McOscar and Henry J. Grabner who declared himself legally of unsound mind in order that he might be committed to a hospital for treatment.

Father Angermaier recovered his health and his normal mind and went about the duties of his priestly office. It was recently brought to his attention that he was legally of unsound mind and still subject to the custody of the county clerk.

He applied for his legal freedom and it was forthcoming.

From "The Fort Wayne News," 2 January 1896, page 3
What Max O'Rell Said of Spittons in America — It Was True — Oxygen Tobacco Cure Was Not Known Then
Max O'Rell, the witty French journalist, who traveled through this country several years ago, said a great many funny things about the American people, and commented on their habits, customs and

manners. His eminence as a writer procured him admission into the most exclusive circles, but he also made it a point to study somewhat, the seamy side of life. Of the furnishings of the American homes he spoke very highly, but there was one adjunct of our households that called forth his utmost jocularity. This was the spittoon.

In the entertaining book he wrote about us called "Johnathan and His Continent" he says: "It is impossible, however, in speaking of American interiors to pass over in silence a certain eyesore which meets you at every turn. The most indispensable, it appears, the most conspicuous at any rate, piece of furniture in America is the spittoon. All rooms are provided with this article of prime necessity; you find one beside your seat in trains; under your table in the restaurants; impossible to escape the sight of the ugly utensil. In the hotel corridors, there is a spittoon standing sentinel outside every door. In public buildings the floors are dotted with them, and they form a line all up the stairs."

He goes on to say that the Americans use them as targets and perform some wonderful feats of marksmanship.

Well, of course this is so. It is somewhat amusing and we cannot deny it in the face of the fact. But we think he could not say this in a few years more. People are trying everywhere to give up the use of tobacco and it seems that with the aid of Oxygen Tobacco Cure they are bound to do it. It is really wonderful what great credit this cure has gained in the short time it has been on the market. Oxygen Tobacco Cure for sale by all druggists.

From "The Fort Wayne News," 27 January 1896, page 2
In view of the multiplied fatalities at Cleveland occasioned by sleepy draw-bridge tenders, it is suggested that some system be devised whereby the trolley cars and fire engines that so frequently plunge through the open draws in that city may have a softer place to alight than the rocky beds of the streams into which they have been falling. A net, like those used beneath trapeze performers at a circus, only composed of cables, is suggested. There is no thought any more of securing the services of watchmen who will keep awake.

From "Reno Evening Gazette," 13 November 1888, page 3
Brevities
Local and General Intelligence
Six new students entered the University yesterday.

Mrs. Rice attempted suicide at Sacramento Friday night.

Many of the boys of the period are like a dilapidated roof—they need shingling.

President Cleveland can now be compared to a tree—he leaves in the Spring, tra-la.

John Lent got in a row at Spokane Falls Friday, and was struck with a cuspidor and killed.

The Carson Republicans are completing their arrangements for a big blowout to-morrow night.

Tim Ryan, a shoemaker at Grimes, Colusa county, Cal., fell into the river yesterday and was drowned.

Two cars of beef cattle were shipped from here yesterday by Irving Ayers to Poley, Heilbron & Co., San Francisco.

The small-pox seems to be making great headway at Portland, Oregon. All the school children are to be vaccinated.

Nearly 100,000 acres of pasture have been converted into small homes in and around Templeton, Cal. within two years.

A fire at Paradise, Nev., Saturday burned the public hall, Proctor's store, Dr. Mack's office and another small building.

From the "Fort Wayne News," 3 March 1904, page 5
Some Conceits of the Day
   Bridge parties were a popular fad on North Hanna and Wagner streets this week.

   DeTanque—"There is unusual activity in Fort Wayne police circles."
   DeSoaque—"Yes, I notice they made a raid last night without waiting for a grand jury indictment."

   It is unfortunate for a man under strict orders from the board of health not to drink city water to be arrested while drinking beer. Jack Dee

From the "Reno Evening Gazette," 31 May 1876, page 2
Decoration Day
   Yesterday the people of these United States were one in remembrance of fallen heroes, in mourning the nation's losses and in offerings of respect upon the graves of buried sons. Within the sound of war we could honor bravery, patriotism and the valiant defense of principles; and now, under the olive branch of peach, it was well to offer respect to the memory of brave men and their gallant deeds. It was an act well-calculated to awaken and strengthen brotherly love; to heal the wounds of a fratricidal war; and above all an act of which manhood should be proud. For amidst the alarms and struggles of war; amidst the victories and defeats, little thought is taken of the tears which follow the fortunes of war. These tears and their memories perpetuate strife and nourish the seeds of future discord. But when friend and foe alike come to the grave, and with uncovered heads unite in mourning a common loss, it is a tribute worthy of heroes. And he is an unworthy citizen who finds himself unable to give equal respect to victor and vanquished, for each lived bravely and died nobly. It is matter for joy that men who fought are first to forget their hatred and mourn the sad results of strife. "The bravest are the tenderest; the loving are the daring," and it fills every manly, patriotic heart to see the land decked with flowers—a bright prophecy for the future—a tribute of love to the heroic dead.

Success is a matter of locality, but this was a touch of heart which made the world akin; and each grave, decorated with expressions of love and regret, is a monument to man's nobility and brotherly love.

Under the sod and the dew, Waiting the judgment day; Tears and love for the blue. Love and tears for the gray.

From the "Fort Wayne News," 22 May 1897
In the Sunday game at Chicago yesterday, a brutal fight between two players, in the presence of the entire audience, was one of the delectable incidents of the Sabbath breaking orgie.

Ambassador Bayard says that he left England "full of conflicting emotions." They say that there is always a choppy sea just outside Queenstown ha[r]bor that makes nearly all the passengers feel that way.

The dispatches from Logansport declare that dishonesty is charged in the case of Banker Johnson. This is too bad. Its getting so now that a banker can't steal half a million of his customers' cash without having his integrity questioned.

From the "Fort Wayne News," 5 October 1895, page 2
Saturday, October 5, 1895

Good evening.

Denizens of infected districts in Chicago are now taking their bacilli hard boiled.

Great Britain has been insulted again. The *Chicago Tribune* speaks of the great game of golf as outdoor tiddledewinks.

There are some good things about these trolley suburban car lines that are run by wind—they don't frighten horses nor injure pedestrians.

The board of health will confer a very great favor upon the community if they succeed in stamping out diphtheria from the several radiating centers established by the holding of public funeral in a case of death from membraneous croup. There is only one way to meet this difficulty; i.e., by prosecuting anybody and everybody responsible for the holding of public funerals in such cases.

The prevalence of diphtheria last winter was directly traceable to this cause of infection, and unless strong methods are taken to prevent, we shall have a repetition of the scourge this year. The ignorance and obstinacy of some physicians and individuals in this regard are simply criminal, and they must be so treated.

From the "Fort Wayne News," 2 February 1897, page 2
After the Elopement

Artie—Darling, you have no idea how anxious I was while you were coming down the rope ladder. I was so afraid you had not fastened it securely above.

Susie—You needn't have been alarmed, dear. Papa tied the knot for me.

From the "Fort Wayne News," 4 January 1898, page 1
Blizzard Has No Terrors

Determined Couple Drive Sixty Miles for a Marriage License.

NILES, Mich., Jan. 4—Charles Gifford, a traveling man, who claims Chicago as his home, and Miss E.M. Johnson, of Eaton Rapids, were so anxious to get married New Year's afternoon that they drove sixty miles in a fierce blizzard and with the mercury below the zero point, to get a marriage license.

On account of the absence of the county clerk at Eaton Rapids, they drove thirty miles to Mason, where they procured the license, and immediately returned home.

The marriage took place late Saturday evening after the couple had been thawed out, it being one of the coldest days of the year.

News and Announcements

Ancestry.com Site Redesign
3 May 2002
Those of you who have visited the site will have noticed some big changes. Along with cheerier colors, the navigation has been made more intuitive and users will find more direct routes to their favorite Ancestry.com products.

As with the previous version, the site is arranged under a series of headers, in the form of buttons this time, on the top of the screen. These headers include:

Home — Home page
Search Records—Search functions, which now goes to a newly designed page which combines the advanced search, search by record type, and search by locality.

Family Trees—The new home of the Ancestry World Tree (AWT), Online Family Tree (OFT), and the Ancestry Family Tree (AFT) downloadable software. Also included on this page in the lower right-hand corner are links to Ancestry.com's selection of free downloadable forms.

Message Boards—A direct link to the Ancestry Message Boards, as well as the Research Registry, where users can let others know what surnames they are researching.

Genealogy Help—This is where you'll find links to columns from the *Ancestry Daily News*, and Ancestry.com columnists. You can also search the Ancestry.com Library, which contains over 5,500 articles to help you locate your ancestors.

Ancestry Shops—A direct link to the great deals on top-quality genealogy products from The Shops @ Ancestry.com.

Ancestry's Online Help Center can now be accessed by clicking on the link at the very bottom of the page that says "Site Help." The database in the Help Center contains answers to hundreds of frequently asked questions about the site, as well as a separate tab for users to submit other questions.

Ancestry will continue to fine-tune the site over the upcoming week, and we hope you'll take a few minutes to browse around the site and acquaint yourself with the new design at <http://www.ancestry.com/rd/home.htm>.

California State Records Access Hearing Set for 7 May

Many of you will remember that last December, Ancestry.com removed the California birth records from our sites. This action was taken in response to reports on hearings in the California State Legislature during which concern was expressed that access to these records could promote identity theft. These hearings were widely reported in the press, raising public outcry, despite the fact that no evidence of such misuse was shown.

Many of you expressed your concern at that time that our removal of these records and the resulting limitation of access to them would be a great loss to the family history community. The California Senate is now considering legislation that would greatly restrict access to these records. That which to date has been available as a matter of law, would be unavailable as a matter of law, except by restricted access through a limited index in California county clerks' offices. The next Senate hearing is set for 7 May 2002. If you are concerned about this loss, and the fact that the legislation, if passed, might mean other states would follow suit, you can contact the relevant Senators and Senate

Committees by sending an e-mail regarding your thoughts.
mailto:senator.bowen@sen.ca.gov
mailto:senator.speier@sen.ca.gov

Desperate Plea From the Editor
9 May 2002
Last Thursday's newsletter contained a notice about the W32.Klez.H@mm worm that is floating around. This virus has recently been upgraded because it is so widespread.

Part of the problem is the virus' ability to spoof e-mail addresses. This means that when someone receives the virus, it may have the address of someone whose computer is clean, but just happens to be in the address book of an infected computer.

On the flip side, if your computer is infected, no one is going to tell you because it does not appear to be coming from you, but rather someone in your address book or in a file on your computer. You will need to scan your system to find out if it is infected.

Please take the time to read about this virus and make certain your computer is clean. I know that about two hundred of you a day are getting infected. Because the worm gathers e-mail addresses from files, as well as address books, it is picking up the e-mail addresses from the newsletter, and our columnists and I are being bombarded with them.

More information about the worm is available at <http://securityresponse.symantec.com/avcenter/venc/data/w32.klez.h@mm.html>.

Regrettably, until the virus dies down, the e-mail addresses found in this newsletter will have a space in them and will not be clickable.

To contact us, either manually copy the address into an e-mail message, or copy/paste them and remove the space.

Wishing you good luck and safe computing!
Juliana

Ancestry.com to Increase Prices 1 June 2002
Subscribe now and Save as Much as 40 Percent
13 May 2002
Ancestry.com will soon be raising subscription prices to its one-of-a-kind collections, so now is the time to subscribe to your favorite data collections and save money before the price increase.

Beginning 1 June prices will be as follows:
Billed Annually

- Super Subscription $189.95 (Includes access to Ancestry's U.S. & Canada Records Collection, U.S. Census Images & Indexes, U.K. & Ireland Records Collection, and Historical Newspapers)
- U.S. Subscription $119.90 (Includes access to Ancestry's U.S. & Canada Records Collection and U.S. Census Images & Indexes)
- U.S. & Canada Records Collection Subscription $79.95
- U.S. Census Images & Indexes Subscription $99.95
- U.K. & Ireland Records Collection $99.95
- Historical Newspapers Collection $79.95

Billed Quarterly

- Super Subscription $99.95 (Includes access to Ancestry's U.S. & Canada Records Collection, U.S. Census Images & Indexes, U.K. & Ireland Records Collection, and Historical Newspapers)
- U.S. Subscription $69.90 (Includes access to Ancestry's U.S. & Canada Records Collection and U.S. Census Images & Indexes)
- U.S. & Canada Records Collection Subscription $29.95
- U.S. Census Images & Indexes Subscription $39.95
- U.K. & Ireland Records Collection $39.95
- Historical Newspapers Collection $29.95

Coming Soon at Ancestry.com

Ancestry.com is working to complete the 1920 Census Index by the end of this month, as well as the posting of all images for the 1930 Census in upcoming months. Efforts are also underway to digitize the 24 million World War I Draft Registration cards held at the National Archives and Records Administration. In addition, work has begun on a significant immigration index that will cover peak immigration years.

Additional databases will continue to be posted each working day with a growing number of them accompanied by images of the original record. In addition, look for increased production in all areas, including the Historical Newspaper Collection.

Besides helping to maintain quality subscription data collections, subscription revenues also go towards maintaining all of the free services at Ancestry.com, RootsWeb.com, and MyFamily.com, which host popular databases, including:

- Ancestry World Tree
- Free Ancestry Family Tree software downloads
- Private Online Family Trees
- Social Security Death Index and other free databases
- Over 24,700 mailing lists
- Over 126,000 message boards containing over 9.7 million posts
- RootsWeb Free Pages and hosted sites
- Free newsletters and online article libraries
- Free downloadable charts and forms
- Research Registry, and much more!

Start your subscription today at:
http://www.ancestry.com/rd/signup.htm

Joint Resolution and Petition from the Federation of Genealogical Societies and the National Genealogical Society
22 May 2002

Please be aware that the National Genealogical Society and the Federation of Genealogical Societies believe strongly that California State Senate Bill 1614 on Vital Records Indexes poses a significant threat to records access in the state of California. These two national organizations have approved and sent the following joint resolution and petition to the Senate Appropriations Committee in California. We encourage you to contact your California Senator to defeat this bill.

Joint Resolution and Petition from
The Federation of Genealogical Societies
and
The National Genealogical Society

The Federation of Genealogical Societies with headquarters in Austin, Texas, a national and international organization of societies, representing fifty-five genealogical societies in California and over 50,000 genealogists and family historians in that state, and further representing 550 societies nationwide with approximately one-half million genealogists and family historians being members of those societies, and

The National Genealogical Society with headquarters in Arlington, Virginia, recognized as the leading genealogical society in the United States and North America, having approximately ten percent of its membership in California, do make the following joint resolution and petition to the legislature of the State of California;

Whereas, California State Senate Bill 1614 on Vital Records Indexes threatens to reduce the information available in the birth and death record indexes rendering them significantly less useful and/or limit the use and access by genealogical researchers and family historians, and

Whereas, both organizations consider these records to be primary to the pursuit of discovering an individual's heritage and history; in fact, central to the human need that answers the yearning deep inside each of us to know who we are and from where we came; and

Essential for the youth of our nation to help develop a sense of their cultural heritage and to provide a strong foundation in a world of shifting values; and

For the youth to research their families and learn, for example, how their families overcame hardships in the past which can give them answers to some of the challenges they face today; and that

This curiosity and need crosses cultural and international boundaries, in a way, uniting us as a human family; and

Whereas, both organizations are equally concerned about the issue of identity theft and are fully supportive of state and local leaders acting responsibly to protect the rights and property of the people they are called to serve,

Do petition the California State legislature to find a balanced solution to the matter of protecting the rights of the citizens of the great State of California from identity theft while still providing sufficient access to the records for the continued use by genealogists and family historians for the legitimate pursuit of tracing ones' heritage and ancestry.

Further, we believe these two objectives are not mutually exclusive and offer the following for your consideration;

According to the First Amendment Coalition, recent studies confirm that most identity thefts occur through the literal theft by friends, relatives, fellow workers or strangers, of wallets, purses or mail, or fraudulent address changes; and

That many of the county recorders do not have the manpower or funding to facilitate the requirements of SB1614 and that the lack of uniformly implementing the proposed bill would render it ineffective for its intended purpose; and

That we understand the powerful tool that mother's maiden name is in uniquely identifying an individual in a given population; that the intersection of two surnames dramatically improves the statistical probability above chance that two individuals are the same person, thus being an extremely useful tool to genealogists and family historians to identify individuals with common surnames within in a given population; and

That this information (particularly mother's maiden name) is readily available in open sources, namely newspapers, especially obituaries, birth and marriage announcements, cemetery tombstones, Who's Who publications, professional directories and published biographies, and

That corporations such as American Express use individual identifiers other than the mother's maiden name which are not found on the vital records indexes, namely the last four digits of the social security number and that due to the open availability of the identity of the maiden name of a person's mother making it readily available for identity theft, that banks and other financial institutions be encouraged to discontinue the use of the mother's maiden name as a unique identifier, and

That the State of California consider adopting legislation

which provides both a level of adequate security and access by genealogists and family historians; and that the legislation from the states of Arizona and/or Kentucky may be used as an appropriate model.

This resolution and petition was adopted by the executives and board of directors of both the Federation of Genealogical Societies and the National Genealogical Society at the annual meeting of the National Genealogical Society held in Milwaukee, Wisconsin, dated 18 May 2002.

Submitted on behalf of the Federation of Genealogical Societies and the National Genealogical Society by:

Dean J. Hunter	Curt B. Witcher
President	President
Federation of Genealogical Societies	National Genealogical Society.

Note: For California Senators' contact information, see <http://www.senate.ca.gov/%7Enewsen/senators/senators.http>.

This bill is slated for a hearing on 23 May, so don't delay in voicing your opinion. Details on the status of the legislation can be found at <http://info.sen.ca.gov/cgi-bin/pagequery?type=sen_bil-info&site=sen&title=Bill+Information>. (Just type SB1614 in the space for "Bill number.")

Research Trip to the Allen County Public Library in Ft. Wayne, IN 22 May 2002

The St. Charles County Genealogical Society and the St. Charles Community College are co-sponsoring a bus trip to the Allen County Public Library in Ft. Wayne, Indiana, with Michael John Neill as the trip genealogist. Trip registrants will have access to a special website to assist them in trip planning and allow all trip registrants to get to know each other. Michael will provide on-site consultation with trip registrants. Those who don't live near suburban St. Louis, Missouri, can drive themselves for a lower price. There's online pre-trip planning, morning lecture sessions at the hotel before the library opens, a Friday night banquet, and more.

Early bird registration deadline had been changed to 31 May 2002. For more information, point your browser to:
http://www.rootdig.com/acpltrip.html

Last Day to Save on Ancestry.com Subscriptions
31 May 2002
Subscribe to Ancestry.com today and save up to 40 percent.
Ancestry.com will be raising subscription prices to its one-of-a-kind collections. Now is the time to subscribe to your favorite data collections and save money before the price increase!

Coming Soon at Ancestry.com
31 May 2002
Ancestry.com expects to complete the 1920 Census Index today with the exception of Puerto Rico, which is in the works. Also, the posting of all images for the 1930 Census should be completed in upcoming weeks.

A new project is underway to digitize the 24 million World War I Draft Registration cards held at the National Archives and Records Administration. In addition, work has begun on a significant immigration index that will cover peak immigration years.

Additional databases will continue to be posted each working day with a growing number of them accompanied by images of the original record. In addition, look for increased production in all areas, including the Historical Newspaper Collection.

Besides helping maintain quality subscription data collections, subscription revenues also go towards maintaining all of the free services at Ancestry.com, RootsWeb.com, and MyFamily.com, which host popular databases, including:

- Ancestry World Tree
- Free Ancestry Family Tree software downloads
- Private Online Family Trees
- Social Security Death Index and other free databases
- Over 24,700 mailing lists
- Over 126,000 message boards containing over 9.7 million posts
- RootsWeb Free Pages and hosted sites

- Free newsletters and online article libraries
- Free downloadable charts and forms
- Research Registry, and much more!

Start your subscription today at:
http://www.ancestry.com/rd/signup.htm

National Archives Announces New Website Design
31 May 2002

Washington, DC. The National Archives and Records Administration (NARA) will launch its website, <http://www.archives.gov>, today, with a dynamic, new look. NARA's former website <http://www.nara.gov> will be merged with <http://www.archives.gov> to form a site that provides online visitors with dramatic improvements in navigation, uniformity, appearance, and accessibility to users with disabilities.

With an eye-catching image of the National Archives Rotunda, the new impact page introduces visitors to the National Archives. The online visitor has immediate access to the website's major topic areas that allow browsing and searching through information about Federal Government records, services provided by the National Archives, and online presentations of exhibits including the Charters of Freedom: the Declaration of Independence, the Constitution, and the Bill of Rights.

Enhancements to the website include:

- Improved Navigation. Web pages will work in intuitive and consistent ways, making it easier for visitors to find what they are looking for and know where they are within the website.
- Improved Look and Feel. Enhanced graphics and the new page layouts will provide visitors with an improved user experience.
- New Features. New features on the website will include print-friendly versions of the Web pages, news and events notices, a drop-down box providing direct access to Web pages, a site index, and an FAQ page.
- Improved Accessibility—The new website is designed to

improve accessibility for people with visual, auditory, or motor impairments. The website is designed so that its content will be available to persons with disabilities who use assisting software to navigate the World Wide Web.

While the appearance and high-level organization of the website is enhanced, the information located on the current website will be available via the new address. Existing bookmarks will be redirected to the new home page or the exact location of the new page.

The National Archives Rotunda is temporarily closed and the Charters of Freedom are off public display. <http://www.archives.gov> will offer visitors a virtual tour of the Charters, information on the project to re-encase the Charters, and updates on the National Archives Building renovation.

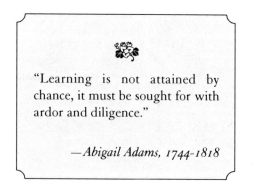

"Learning is not attained by chance, it must be sought for with ardor and diligence."

—*Abigail Adams, 1744-1818*

Quick Tips

Safety First

Keep Your Genealogy Safe from Loss or Damage
Expanding on Margie's Quick Tip from 20 May 2002
   (See   <http://www.ancestry.com/rd/prodredir.asp?sourceid= 831&key=A576702>.)
   I too was fearful about losing my genealogy research. I studied purchasing a large safe. When I couldn't find one that was large enough to hold all my research, I searched for something effective at an office supply store. I then found a fireproof four-drawer file cabinet. The price is about the same as a small- to medium-sized safe, but it has so much more room, a lock, a key, and is very heavy. I keep all my genealogy files, backup disks, photos, etc., in this file cabinet.
   I live in South Louisiana, so another fear is hurricanes. When I know one is coming our way, I transfer all my files, photos, etc., into files boxes and load them into my car. If I (or anyone else) leaves, so does my research. One time, when a hurricane came a little to close for comfort, I packed all my genealogy files and sent them with my daughter, who was leaving. After she left, I realized that I hadn't given one thought to sending insurance policies, bonds, jewelry, etc. You can guess where my priorities lie.

                                                              —*K. Licciardi*

Keeping Records Safe from Disaster

After last week's tornado in La Plata, MD, and after the F-5 tornado on 28 April 2002, I feel doubly blessed. I was on the road in La Plata, MD at the time it hit, and it missed the car I was in by about a half mile (I saw it pass behind us and cross the road). When we finally made it home, it had missed our house, too, but only by a few hundred yards. We hadn't seen any warnings of the imminent tornado watches because we hadn't watched the TV or listened to the radio all weekend, and there is no siren warning system currently in Charles County.

After seeing the tornado's aftermath first-hand, several thoughts ran through my mind. The one pertaining to my genealogy was incredibly frightening. Had the tornado destroyed our house, as it did many others, the only thing likely to be standing afterward is the safe we have bolted to the foundation of the house. All my genealogy work, including irreplaceable family photos, newspaper clippings, etc., are on the first floor in our house, with some stuff in a two-drawer filing cabinet that doesn't even lock! I'm seriously considering moving my "genealogy office" down to the basement, and keeping all my sentimental goodies in the safe, where they can't be harmed by any disaster.

It's terribly sad to see people still looking through debris in La Plata for their personal belongings, knowing that some may never be found. Incredible as it may seem, some things from La Plata are apparently being found across the Chesapeake Bay in Dorchester County, MD, having been carried there by the tornado. I'm hoping that people who find these items can identify their owners and return them somehow. I guess the saying "location, location, location" doesn't only pertain to real estate—it also pertains to where you keep your irreplaceable belongings.

— Margie Pasini

Cemetery Warning

In reply to the 25 May 2001 Quick Tip, "Cemetery Warning," it is always advisable to pre-set your cell phone to 911 in the event you need to call for police assistance or other emergency. This way one does not have to go about punching numbers, just the send button will get the assistance to you. One of my friends has a business in the more desolate parts of the Viuex Carre of New Orleans. When she must leave late at night or on desolate weekends daylight hours she has her cell phone preset to 000 and laying on the passenger side of her car. Just passing on a great safety idea.

—*John Cordero*

Note: Since many of us may be visiting cemeteries at this time of year, I am reprinting the above-referenced warning from last year:

Anyone planning on visiting a cemetery should be especially wary at this time of year. Mother's Day, Memorial Day, and Father's Day see an increase in visitors to the cemetery.

Thieves know this, too. This makes cemetery visitors an appealing target for theft. Whenever you visit the cemetery it's a good idea to follow some common sense safety precautions:

- Don't leave your purse or other valuables in your car.
- If possible, go with a group.
- Go during the daylight hours.
- If you have a cell phone, it is also a good idea to bring it with you so that you can call for help if necessary. Stay safe!

More on Cell Phone Safety
I have an additional follow-up on the cell phone suggestion <http://www.ancestry.com/rd/prodredir.asp?sourceid=831&key=A 570802>. Rather than keeping the cell phone on the seat of the car, I keep it on my body. If there were an accident or if I had to stop quickly, the cell phone could be out of reach, either because it flew somewhere else in the car, or if I had to make a quick exit, or were pinned behind the wheel, etc.

—*Martha Backstrom*

Visiting Cemeteries

Record Latitude and Longitude in Cemeteries
I recommend adding degrees of latitude and longitude when describing the location of a cemeteries and obscure burial sites.

Lat/Lon allows pinpointing locations within mere feet. It is especially helpful in finding an accurate location of grave sites in rural areas, many of which are unmarked, overgrown, abandoned, and may only contain one or two graves.

A Global Positioning System (GPS) device can be purchased for well under $100. Pawn Shops are a good source. They're simple and easy to use. Just turn them on at the site you want to record, and within a minute or so the degrees of lat/lon are displayed.

Try it. I believe that in the future, genealogy buffs and other researchers will appreciate this bit of extra effort on our part. I sure wish my ancestors had passed this kind of information on to me.

—*[Unsigned]*

Tape Recorder Tips
One thing that I have found most helpful when researching my family tree is a little $20 tape recorder. I purchased three additional tapes, so my total investment was under $25.

I always carry the recorder with me. I can talk as I walk through cemeteries, and give exact directions to the gravesite I am researching. If I am in a library and there is no copy machine handy, I can dictate in a soft whisper the information from an obituary or a newspaper event. Often times, something I have seen or heard will raise some questions in my mind, and I can also "leave myself a memo" to check into a certain thing when I have time.

Transcribing my notes does not take long, and I know that I will not have forgotten something that I need for my research. This is the best little investment I ever made.

—*Leora Lee*

Enjoy the View
If and when you are at a cemetery, take a minute to survey the location. Often, the old cemeteries have lovely locations, sometimes on the side of a hill, and you can see for a distance; or a few graves will be placed under some large trees, with the river down below. I have enjoyed walking in cemeteries in both the Northwest and the Midwest.

—*Elsie Wilson*
Oregon

Photograph Cemetery Landmarks

When I go to a cemetery, I not only take photos of tombstones, I also take photos of the church and, if available, photos of pillars or archways that lead into the cemetery. This not only is a landmark for me on my sojourns on tombstone searches, but there may also be information inscribed on a plaque in front of, or on the church, or on the pillars or archways at the entrance. There may be a monument within the cemetery itself with valuable information on it. As for me, I really enjoy looking for evidence of my ancestor's existence and as much information that I can collect when I am in my "in search of mode," for my unknown ancestors.

— *Laura LaRose,*
Boswell, Pennsylvania

Address Labels for Cemetery Photos

I take a lot of cemetery photos. It's easy to forget which cemetery a photo was taken in, so I use address labels. I print a sheet with the name of the cemetery, the town, county, state. This way, I can quickly and easily attach the label to the back of the photo. It's so much faster than hand writing the name and address on the back.

— *Dianne Duncan*
Kingston, Washington

Trouble Free Cemetery Labels

I take lots and lots of cemetery photos. Here's a tip for trouble-free labeling: I write on a white page on a clipboard in DARK FELT TIP, the name of the cemetery and the CITY/STATE (and location number if there is enough space to write) all clearly and large enough to show up in my photo. Then religiously, I put the card at the base of the monument on either the WEST or the NORTH position to the marker. I only deal with WEST or NORTH and so West would be to the Left of the monument, North would be to the Right of the monument. EVERY photo I take is immediately identifiable. I don't need labels or a pen. I can use the photos the second they come out of the photo envelope.

— *Valentine*

Diagrams Make Finding Headstones a Snap

I go a step further than Dianne suggested in a previous quick tip. I photograph the entry to the cemetery or the church where it is located. I also draw a quick sketch showing the orientation of the cemetery and the location (row and plot) of my ancestor's grave(s). That way, I can find them quickly on any return visit or direct other family members to their location.

—*Ila Verne Toney*
Conroe, Texas

Taking Cemetery Photos

I take a lot of cemetery photos. I always take a photo of the entrance or church, also the section, as often there are signs telling which section they are in. I also use my computer and label the photos when I put them in my album.

—*Joe Cawley*
Augusta, Georgia

Write It Down

This "tip" is probably a common one, but quite useful: Take pictures of headstones and write on the back of the picture all the additional information necessary to know where these headstones are located, such as the name of the cemetery, city, county and state where located, lot number, section, etc. if known. Also, if name is not present or legible, write it on the back of the picture. For example, sometimes there will be a big family stone with small stones that say "Mother," "Father," etc. If the pictures of the big stone and smaller stones were to become separated later, you or someone else will know whose grave you/they are looking at. Keep an alphabetized index file in a recipe style box of these pictures so you can readily located them.

—*Susan Pena*
Arlington, Texas

Camera Lens Helps Read Stones

Recently, I was in a cemetery on a rainy day looking for my ancestor's gravestones. When I found the gravestones, several were difficult to read because of the wear on them with the passing of time and the exposure to bad weather. I wanted to photograph them anyway, and when I put the camera to my eye I discovered that I could make out some of the lettering and numbers on some of the stones a little better than with my naked eye. My husband suggested that it might have something to do with the filtering of light through the lens. I don't know what it was, but it helped me to make out the name Eliza on one particular stone that was badly decayed. Maybe this will work for others, too.

—Sherry Kilgore

Contact Current Plot Owner
I was recently in Ohio for a funeral. While there, I was checking the cemetery records in the office, when I came across a name that had not been there on an earlier trip. It turned out to be the name and address of the current owner of the lot where my husband's great-grandfather was buried. She was the daughter of my husband's great-uncle and when I contacted her she was able to provide information on other family members. This woman was born in 1913 and had a great deal of personal knowledge about the family.

—Janet Moorhead

Searching for Names

Difficulties with Ethnic Surnames
Regarding Tony Hansen's tip to try various spellings of first and last names in searches <http://www.ancestry.com/rd/prodredir.asp?sourceid=1644&key=A570802>, ethnic surnames can also pose difficulties. Suffixes can change depending on the gender, or if the name denotes a couple. Example: My mother's surname appears as both Marolewski and Marolewska (the female version of the name). There are other suffixes that are not properly part of a name at all, but under which one might be listed in an index.

—Linda Herrick Swisher
Hobart, Indiana

Search Tips

When searching databases, everyone knows you should try various spellings of the last name. However, don't forget to also try out various spellings of the first name, in the last name field. One of my grandparents had his name reversed in the Ellis Island database, and it was misspelled as well.

Also, you can't trust consistency across relatives. Another relative proved hard to find in the Ellis Island database because of this. He and his three siblings who came through Ellis Island all used their Norwegian farm name as their last name. But, unlike the others, on the ship's manifest, he used only his patronymic name.

— Tony Hansen

Alternate Spellings of Names

Locating Hispanic ancestors in U.S. Census records and finding aids can often be a frustrating experience. Original census records and finding aids (databases and indexes) often contain typographical errors or phonetic spellings that can complicate online searching. Searching under alternate spellings sometimes yields correct results, but what do you do when even this fails? Searching under first name and county might not be practical especially if this yields too many results, so consider the possibility that your male Hispanic ancestor may be listed under his maternal surname!

Take the case of Librado Garza Garcia and his family who appear in the 1920 U.S. Census, Texas, Starr Co., ED 157, Justice Precinct 4, sheet 1A. From other sources, I knew that Librado's father was Andres GARZA and his mother was Jacinta GARCIA, but my initial search in the 1920 census indexes failed. By searching for him under his mother's surname, I successfully located the correct census image listing his family.

In the 1920 U.S. Census, Librado incorrectly appears on line 15 under is mother's surname as "GARCIA Librado G" followed by his wife, Josefa, and their unmarried children: Marta, Florencio, Daniel, Benjamin, and Josefina. By analyzing all the names of family members, I determined that this was indeed the Librado Garza Garcia who married Josefa Garza Escobar.

A closer examination of the entire census sheet shows that the next family listed (beginning on line 22) is that of Librado and Josefa's son, Andres. Andres' surname is correctly given as "GARZA," and the names of his wife and children also agree with the data from my other sources.

Lesson learned: When searching for Hispanic ancestors, try searching under the person's maternal surname if the paternal surname doesn't retrieve the correct results.

—Irma (Salinas) Holtkamp

Check for Illogical Misspellings
With the help of Soundex, I have found several variations of the surname "Jeudevine" that I am researching. When I accidentally discovered that it was also listed as "Jendevine," I received valuable information that I was previously missing.

Transcribers had difficulty interpreting the cursive writing on some documents and had mistaken the "U" for an "N". "Louie" became "Lonie" in another document. Also, "E" and "I" can be confusing to transcribers.

Consider cursive letters that may be misread and check for illogical misspellings of the surnames you are researching.

—Jennifer Cochran
Las Vegas, Nevada

More on Post Office Names
On 9 April, a Quick Tip warned that the place where the mail was delivered might not be the name of a town. For example, "Potter's Store, Alabama" might actually be a store owned by Mr. Potter, the postmaster in an area where there was no incorporated town; or "Potter's Crossing" could be the crossroads where the post office was located, and not the name of a town.

In the olden days, there were many little "crossroads" in rural areas that are now parts of larger towns and major cities in Europe as well as North America.

Today, we also find that postal delivery areas frequently cross the boundaries from what is now one suburban town and go into the next suburban town, because the delivery areas for the post offices were mapped out when the land between towns was just open country belonging to neither town. And so those residents of Summit may now have mail addresses and zip codes for Evanstown, or vice versa.

Mail addresses to not need to correspond to legal addresses or to town boundary lines. Today, as centuries ago, "city" or "town" on the mailing address simply indicate the name or location of that post office which was assigned many years ago to handle the mail for the particular piece of land in question—no matter what town it is in. Likewise, if your post office should close, your mail will be sent to another post office in another town for delivery to you, and it had better have the correct name and zip code for that post office, never mind the town in which you reside!

—*E. Shelly*

Search Databases with the First Name
If you are not having much luck when searching on Ancestry.com's engine for the census, try searching by first names if you have a good feel for where they lived. I found several people in the 1920 census this way when the surname was incorrect, either in the index or on the census itself.

—*John S. Chapman*

Use a Space When Searching "Mc" Names
I received help from your technical support staff and thought that that help could be worthy of a tip. I was looking for McBrides in the 1850 Census and knew they existed in the place which I was searching because I had the actual sheet I had copied from a NARA visit- but I couldn't find them on your search engine. The solution was to put a space between the "Mc" and "Bride." Perhaps most people know this, but I didn't and I spent a lot of hours in this endeavor until I received this advice.

—*Lynn Vardakis*

Ellis Island Secrets
Haven't checked the Ellis Island database yet (<http://www.ellisisland.org>)? Think your ancestors came earlier, so they didn't stop there? That's what I used to think until I checked the registry

on a whim and found thirteen entries for the surname I was researching. Though the family had not immigrated during the time Ellis Island was in operation, they took several trips abroad coming through Ellis Island when returning home and some of the family were even crew members on the ship. One man was listed three times as a crewmember on different ships. Don't be afraid to check different registries even though you think they weren't there.

— Sherida Childers

Soundex on the Internet
I thought of this quick tip when I was reading Juliana Smith's "Search Strategy" column in the 6 May 2002 *Ancestry Daily News*.

Some time ago I downloaded a freeware Soundex generator (dated 1994). I have used it on occasion. I figured there might be newer and better ones out there, so I used Google.com to search for Soundex. I found several online Soundex generators, including this one at RootsWeb.com:

<http://resources.rootsweb.com/cgi-bin/soundexconverter>

Or go to the RootsWeb.com home page and select Soundex Converter under their "Tools and Resources." When a result is displayed, it also lists all names it has with the same Soundex code. I used my maternal grandmother's maiden name, Dwyer, since Ms. Smith used the same name. The code is D600, and they list twenty-two names with the same Soundex code.

I also found a freeware downloadable Soundex generator, with a few extra features. It's called ShowSoundex. The link to download it is:

<http://www.sog.org.uk/cig/software/index.html>

The author is Barney Tyrwhitt-Drake. His webpage has a summary of its features:

<http://www.tdrake.demon.co.uk/soundex.htm>

It can handle two names at a time, and has an option of from three to seven characters of Soundex results.

— Tom McGourin

Paperwork

Use Archival Products for Labeling

I, too, used to label the photos of gravestones to identify not only the cemetery with city and state, but also the relationship to the common ancestor of the individual and myself. After having done many this way, I learned that adhesive labels were not ideal. It took a librarian who needed acid-free paper to tell me this, though I worked in a college in-house printing operations shop.

It should be stressed that labels and any papers and photo album pages should be acid free. The label adhesive should also be one that is safe to use on photos, otherwise the properties of the adhesive can start seeping through and damage the photo or the album page and the photos and/or images on the other side of that page. The same holds for photo mounting corners.

It's better to use an acid-free pencil or ink pen and carefully write on the back of the photo the information you desire to record. Photo album supplies such as the acid-free pens, pencils, papers, album pages, and other accessories can be found more readily now than ten to fifteen years ago. Wal-Mart and other like stores, as well as stationery stores such as Hallmark, have a range of these supplies at reasonable prices.

—Debbi Geer

Keeping Images with Transcriptions

To keep a census image together with your transcription, simply print the image and then print a blank census form for that year onto the back side of the same piece of paper. You can print a shot of just the part you want or the entire sheet. I use high quality print mode. Sometimes, I print a shot of the part I want on a landscape printer setting to get it as big as it will go on the paper, for easier reading later.

That way, you can have a copy of the source on the same sheet of paper as your transcription. I do the transcription from the screen directly onto the census form. Those with poor handwriting can scan the census form and then add transcribed text to the form.

— Cindy Espinoza
Grand Junction, Colorado

Make Copies of Obituaries

When I go to a library to locate obituaries I prefer to make a copy of the obituary and then write the newspaper name and date on the copy. When I get home I type the obituary as it appears (including any errors) in a word document and categorized it into one of several family surname files for quick access later.

However, there are times when obtaining a copy of the obituary is simply impossible because of a lack of reader-printers. In this case, I developed my own form, to make sure I extract all the information I need from the obituary. I keep a blank form on my computer and make copies as necessary. I don't worry about wasting time, leaving anything out, or waiting for a reader-printer. This is also great when my husband is with me, as the form is self-explanatory. Even a child who is able to read the obituary can use it and help, but I make sure I give them obituaries that will be easy to find.

— Debbi Geer

Citing Books

When researching at a library or wherever I make a copy from a book. I write on the back of the copy (in pencil) the name of the library and city and state that I made the copy. I also copy the title page and make a note of the reference place at the library. Then if I have to "prove" my source to someone, I have it handy.

— Iris F. Harris

Spring Cleaning Tip

As I began the "spring cleaning" of my paper files and then updating electronic files, I found it quite helpful to pencil in (on the paper files) the date and initials of who/when the update occurred. This not only lets me know the information has been dealt with, but also the date that each individual file was worked on. It also allows me to keep track of new information, which may have been "filed" but not truly "added" to the system. I use this to check for duplication and interfamilial connections.

—Judith Schwab

Save Time with Pre-punched Paper
I got in the habit of hole punching the paper that came out of my printer until I went to an office supply store one day to buy printer paper. I discovered there is a company (Williamette) that has paper conveniently punched with the three holes. Now, when I know I will be filing research into the family notebook I use this paper, and when I am filing to other sources, I use unpunched paper. The price is the same for both types of paper.

—Charee R

Word Watch

Whose Language Is It, Anyway?
Have you discovered a stone with an unusual transcription on it, or perhaps a very brief note that you have come to believe is written in a foreign tongue and needs translation?

Don't be too quick to jump to that conclusion! Take a few moments to examine the matter more closely.

Consider, for example, this inscription that came from an old, partly broken and faded tombstone I was asked to decipher.

Although some of the characters that had been chiseled into the stone did look a bit unusual, I realized they were just A's and I's, nonetheless. The inscription read:

```
1745
MARIA OPTIGRAFF B__  <—Missing
BIIN BARIT HIR
THA 3 FA AF
AGOST BIIN ATEN
EARS AF AJH
```

This puzzle had been considered by a number of researchers before me. It had been presumed the inscription was some sort of Dutch or German. I could not accept that. So I thought and thought about it and found myself muttering the inscription as I imagined a Dutch or German immigrant would say it.

AJH resembling AGE. AGOST sounded like AUGUST. BARIT HIR became BURIED HERE. The entire inscription became—

1745
MARIA OPTIGRAFF BORN?
BEING BURIED HERE
THE 3- TH OF
AUGUST BEING EIGHTEEN
YEARS OF AGE

It was just Broken English! Broken English of a "flavor" harmonizing with the nationality of the deceased—not German or Dutch at all.

So "whose language is it anyway?" If you stop and think about it, it just might be yours!

—*Vince Summers*

Those Little Things That Make a Difference

Include Full Location & Names on Posts
When reading an article or checking an inquiry, many times it will state the name of the town (i.e., Happy Hollow), but no state, county, or country. Without knowing if it is near the town or area I am searching I don't have anything to go on. My tip is to always include more information and not just a name of a town.

—*Berniece N. Moore*

Browse Through Lists a Second Time
This tip follows the one given in the 20 May column <http://www.ancestry.com/rd/prodredir.asp?sourceid=831&key=A

576608>. While it is a good idea to check the archives when you join a list, it is also a good idea to occasionally go back and browse through the archives again. Obviously you would want to do this when you discover a new line. But even if you have been watching a list for a while, you can miss something. (Like before that first cup of coffee kicks in!) Also, you may find that you overlooked something because you didn't have a firm date or name the first time you saw it.

— Terri

RAOGK Tip

This tip is for all of you who volunteer for "Random Acts Of Genealogical Kindness" (RAOGK —<http://members.aol.com/dearmyrtle/99/990307.htm>).

I keep a special RAOGK folder. On the left side, I keep each pending "case" with copies of all e-mail requests, my responses as to any estimated timeframes, any copying costs, further questions, suggestions for the best way to deal with each request, etc. Each case is paper clipped together from the most recent backwards, to make leafing through it easy when I get to the library for my monthly lookup trip.

On the right side, stapled together are completed "cases" with copies of documents found and sent to the person who made the request, any more correspondence, advice on further research, etc. Then, when I do my own research, or am doing other volunteering or whatever, I take the folder along in case I come across something I think one of these persons could use. I have everything right in front of me so I can make a quick copy, or notation for them. I also have the e-mail address there to contact the person again. Then, I don't have to say, "Darn, I wish I could tell so and so about the biography I found in a hanging file with the surname this person is researching."

It has come in handy several times, and there is nothing we genealogists like better than helping others with their research.

— Sherry Broussard

Saved Medical Miscellany Helps A Healthy History

I was lucky enough to be the one to go through my folks' things when they both died. One of the things I saved and plan to use in my medical genealogy are all the medical bills, prescriptions, notes, and whatnot. These bits of information are helpful in reconstructing at what age a disease or illness occurred; when accidents happened; where the folks were when these things happened, and a myriad of other information. It is great for family alerts as we get our physicals. Of course, the costs are a humorous aspect compared to today's medical expenses. It is always easy to throw things out later, but nearly impossible to retrieve them.

—Karen T.

Making Magnified Images Readable

Recently, I have discovered that after magnifying images one or two times, the text can appear too dark, too bold, smeared, or will bleed together. Thus, items I print normally become practically unreadable. By accident, I've found that if I change my printer setting to economy (Epson), in most cases, but not always, the text suddenly becomes clear and easily readable again. It appears the imaging content or the printers cannot clearly handle DPIs of 360 and up. Some of my friends have the same problem.

—E.L. Durr

Maps

Map Making Resources Make Searches Easier

I am currently researching in my home state of Iowa. I grew up there, but have been gone since 1958. While working on my census reports, I found many new Townships which I didn't remember. I guess I didn't pay that much attention to things like that. So, I went to <http://www.topozone.com> and made a map of my home county of Des Moines County, as well as all the immediate counties around—Lee, Louisa, Henry, and since Des Moines County falls on the Mississippi River. I also printed some maps of Illinois.

The project took a while, but this was a fun craft. I taped all the pages together, and then taped it to the wall near my computer. When I go into my census reports now, I can check the map, and see where I am. When I find a family member in a census report, I go to the map and mark it with their name and year of census. Each of the Townships are already on the map, I just highlighted them with a colored marker, and also darkened the borders on the counties. This helped my old eyes a bit.

When I finished making this map, and found how handy it was, I then went to <http://www.mapquest.com> and looked up my hometown of Burlington, Iowa. And yes, you guessed right, I made a large street map of it. It's also hanging on the wall.

I discovered some interesting things while going through the 1910 and 1920 Census. Since most of the Iowa censuses have added street names, you can trace where your families lived. Did they still remain in the same location over the years or were they constantly moving?

My mother was only one year old during the 1910 Census and eleven years old during the 1920 census period. I discovered that her family lived in the same place, and her first husband lived within a five-minute walk from her family home. Her third husband lived halfway between both of them. Of course they didn't know each other. Her third husband, my father, was married and had a family already. In fact, the home he lived in was two doors down from where I grew up as a child. And today the house she grew up in still stands. I have relatives still living there.

I mark my street map also, and I know where most of my relatives lived at the beginning of the 20th Century. They all lived close in proximity—most of them in walking distance. All were close to the Oak Street Baptist Church that was started by my German ancestors. I've discovered a lot about my family, things I never knew while growing up, just by making a couple of maps and keeping track of their movements over the years. I wish some of the earlier census reports were as helpful as the later ones.

Oh, and by the way, on my large county map, there are also some of the cemeteries listed in the area. I know most of my family was buried in Aspen Grove Cemetery, but I had other family that was buried, near where they lived their last years. I have also marked these on my county map.

—Dottie Stokes
Working on her LOHMANN, BRUMM, FEHSE families, and
many, many more.

Labeling Photographs

More Photo Labeling Tips

When faced with labeling a large group photo, where individuals may not be lined up in neat rows, here is one solution I've hit upon.

- Put the photo in an archival sheet protector.
- Using an archival pen (fade proof, water proof, acid free -I find mine at art supply stores), draw an oval or circle around each face.
- Number each person, placing the number where it can be seen against clothing or background, but not on the face.
- On a separate sheet of acid free paper, make a list of the numbers and, next to them, where available, the names of known people.
- If you don't know everyone, but want to share the photo with others who may be able to help, make quality scanned or color laser copies of the photo and hand copy another sheet protector.When labeling any photo, I use hints I learned from a rare book librarian. In addition to using an archival pen, she told me never to write in the area behind the faces and to try to choose a dark area of the photo. Then, should the ink somehow manage to migrate through the paper, even though it shouldn't if it is archival, it will not bleed through to such a distracting or important part of the picture.

Another possibility is to put the information on acid free paper and then to tape it to the photo using archival tape.

—Susan Hopkins

Naming Digital Photos

Computer genealogy programs use a unique ID number for each individual. Use that ID number, plus a suffix of some sort if you have more than one photo of the individual.

Or, as in the stated example, use the first letter of the last name, plus the ID number from your genealogy program, and then a suffix (like 01 or A). If John Smith has an ID of 80 in your database, then his digital photo would be S8001.xxx, where the xxx is the extension associated with your digital photo program.

As long as your original file names are less than eight characters long, you will have no more problems with truncation of long file names when you perform a restore.

Don't forget to print out a listing of the people in your database to use as a reference.

—Dawn Bingaman

Interviewing

Preparing for an Interview

When conducting an "interview" with a relative, spend some time becoming familiar with his or her background before you try to look at the world though his or her eyes. Who is your relative's parents, nieces, uncles, grannies, cousins? What period of history did the relative live though? When the relative talks about Auntie Flo's husband who was killed in the war, you won't waste any time working out that it is in fact the husband of Dorothy Mavis Florence Butterworth, who must have been involved in WW1. So often, these connections are made after the interview, whereas realizing this at the time will lead you to many more questions and areas for investigation.

—Mike Johns
Sydney, Australia

Interview Older Family Members

This may be a repeat "tip" by someone else. It is such a simple, but useful tip.

I made copies of old pictures that my mother, now deceased, had in her album, and sent them to Mother's first cousins that are still living. I asked these cousins to identify everyone they can in the picture. Sometimes I write on the back of the picture the people I know, and leave blank the ones I don't know. Some of the children in the pictures, now grown, have been identified by these cousins.

They knew them when they were children. This has helped me identify other pictures of these children that are in the family.

I have also called some of these cousins, and they have told me little things of interest like "your great-grandmother and her sister were 'Corseteers' at Marshall Fields in Chicago. They were certified in this profession." This may not sound too exciting but they don't have corsets anymore and I had no idea my great-grandmother worked at Marshall Fields in Chicago, nor that her sister did either.

My point is, you can find out all kinds of information that may lead to bigger and better pieces of information by interviewing older family members. For example, the time period that my great grandmother and her sister lived in Chicago can be calculated and then the census records and directories can be used to determine their address, children, husband's name, etc. especially if you don't have that information and are seeking to find it. Interviewing older relatives that are still alive is a wonderful resource in itself. It can be done over the phone or in person. In person, you can get a picture of them as they look today for your records also.

—Susan Pena
Arlington, Texas

New Genealogical Helps

Voice Recognition Software for Transcribing Tasks

Faced with the task of transcribing a number of old hand-written letters so that they could be annotated and easily made available to others, I purchased voice recognition software (Via Voice, $70) and read the letters into my word processor. The software "trains" itself to understand your voice. After the first few letters were read, the error rate decreased significantly, taking much of the drudgery out of the whole typing process.

—Barry McGhan
Ann Arbor, Michigan

New Anglo Italian Mailing List

I set up the Anglo Italian Mailing list, which is hosted by RootsWeb.com, in January 2002. This was to be a discussion forum for those of us in the UK researching our Italian ancestry, but it became apparent, very early on, that a more formal society was needed. Through the mailing list, a small group of us gathered "virtually" together and set about organizing a formal Anglo Italian Family History Society. We had an Inaugural meeting at the venue for the Society of Genealogist Fair, here in the UK on 4 May 2002, which was well attended. The Anglo Italian Family History Society was then formally launched. We welcome and encourage new members. We are currently organizing and planning various transcription projects to aid fellow Anglo Italian Researchers.

A membership form is available for downloading via:
<http://www.dreamwater.net/anglersrest/aifhsform.htm>

The Society webpage is still under construction, but the mailing list page is available via:
<http://www.dreamwater.net/anglersrest/Italian.htm>

For any further information please send e-mail to the address at the bottom of this page. ("Anglers Rest")

—Julie Goucher

Fast Facts

Make Your Voices Heard

Last month, we asked you to answer our "Reader's Voices" question for the March/April issue of *Ancestry* Magazine. Thanks for all the great responses—see what you said on page eight of the May/June issue. The May/June issue asks this question: "What record collection would you like to see online? Why?" Send an e-mail to mailto:ameditor@ancestry.com (subject line: Reader's Voices) and let us know what record collections you are interested in. Include your name, what city, and what state you are from. Your answer could be featured in the next issue of *Ancestry* Magazine. You are also welcome to make comments on other articles in our magazine. Just send your e-mail to the address above.

Civil War Research Database

The Civil War Research database, available online to Ancestry.com Data Subscribers, has the digitized, indexed, and interlinked roster records of 2,100,000 soldiers (out of approximately 4 million who served), 2,719 regimental chronicles, 1,010 officer profiles, 3,343 battle synopses, and 1,012 soldier photographs to date. When you find your ancestor, the database provides you with enlistment information, and the regiment in which he served. By clicking on the regiment, you can get more information about the regiment including battles fought, arranged chronologically. Click on highlighted battles for even more information. In addition, there is a link to the list of other soldiers in the regiment.

Ancestry.com Data Subscribers can search the Civil War Research database at:

<http://www.ancestry.com/search/rectype/military/cwrd/main.ht>

You can subscribe to Ancestry.com at <http://www.ancestry.com/rd/signup.htm> or by calling 1-800-ANCESTRY (1-800-262-3787)

Step-by-Step Family History Online Guide
New to family history research? Check out *Ancestry* Magazine's step-by-step guide to family history! The series, called "Family History Made Easy: Step by Step" and written by Terry and Jim Willard, is available in the Ancestry.com Library at:

<http://www.ancestry.com/rd/prodredir.asp?sourceid=831&key=A208213>

Genealogy Online Training Courses
- Search more than 1 billion names at Ancestry.com with a thirty day subscription, including our online census images
- Receive four weeks of lessons and interaction with a genealogy expert
- Interact with a genealogy expert on each lesson through the site message board
- Receive tips and advice on how to find ancestors online
- Learn from eight independent study lessons through site interaction and worksheets for only $29.95 (that's less than $4 per lesson!)
- Create your family tree using Online Family Tree software and downloadable genealogy forms
- Collaborate with other site members to grow your family tree over the course of a year

See <http://www.myfamily.com/isapi.dll?c=home&htx=gen-training>.

Royal Irish Constabulary

Genealogists tirelessly search for records that will open the doors to undiscovered family history. Though vital records are often the most promising source, there are many different record types that provide us with the information central to our discoveries.

Ancestry has recently acquired an index of the Royal Irish Constabulary. Created in 1816, the Royal Irish Constabulary was the first 'Royal' police force in the British Empire. The details of all individuals who enlisted in the Constabulary between 1816 and 1921 are included in this database. The index includes vital information such as the name, a year of birth or an age on enlistment as well as selected comments. The microfilm reference numbers are also provided for easy access to the original documents.

With the facts contained in this index as well as the particulars provided in the original documents, these records are sure to disclose information vital to your research as well as provide insight to the lives of your relatives. Click here to discover your roots.
<http://www.ancestry.com/rd/redir.asp?sourceid=1381&targetid=3564>

See Your Ancestor's Photo in Ancestry Magazine

Would you like to see a photo of your ancestors in *Ancestry* Magazine? Submit your favorite photos to the "Photo Corner." Submissions should include your name, contact information, date of photo, who is pictured, and a short description. Please do not submit a photo of living persons without written consent. Mail a quality duplicate (no photocopies or originals) to *Ancestry* Magazine. P.O. Box 990, Orem, UT 84057, or e-mail a 300 DPI TIFF scan to mailto:ameditor@ancestry.com with "Photo Corner" in the subject line. Submissions become the property of *Ancestry* Magazine. You will be contacted if your photo is chosen.

Ancestry Family Tree—Free Software
With Ancestry Family Tree You Can:

- Organize all your family history information in one convenient gathering place.
- Zero in on your ancestors in Ancestry.com's valuable databases as they are entered (or downloaded) into the family tree software with the software's powerful search tool.
- Ancestry World Tree files are also automatically searched and once located and verified, whole branches of your family tree can be automatically imported into your tree.
- Attach important files, documents, even photos to your online tree, making a comprehensive history your family will cherish.
- Easily share your family tree with other family members around the world via the Internet, and collaborate online!

Easy to Use

The software is very intuitive and easy to use. Here's how it works:

1. Members can download the software *free* at Ancestry.com.
2. Enter a name to start with, in the space provided in the software's simple interface. For increased results, add parents' names as well.
3. Once you've entered this beginning data, Ancestry Family Tree immediately begins searching more than 1.2 billion records at Ancestry.com and returns likely matches for each. Results are ranked for accuracy, so it's easy to find the right data.

Download your own copy of Ancestry Family Tree today:
<http://www.ancestry.com/rd/redir.asp?targetid=3286&sourceid=831>

Look for Ancestry.com at NGS Conference in Milwaukee
If you're planning on attending the National Genealogical Society's Conference in Milwaukee next week, be sure to stop by the Ancestry.com booth. Ancestry.com representatives will be giving free demos of the various features available at Ancestry.com,

MyFamily.com, and RootsWeb.com between sessions. Please stop by and say hello! We'd love to see you.

For more information about the NGS Conference in Milwaukee, go to:

<http://www.ngsgenealogy.org/>

Samuel Clemens (AKA Mark Twain) in the 1880 Census

Ancestry.com subscribers with access to the Census Collection can see the enumeration for Samuel Clemens, better known as Mark Twain, in Connecticut in 1880. Just go to: <www.ancestry.com/search/rectype/census/usfedcen/main.htm>

- 1880 U.S. Federal Census
- Connecticut
- Hartford
- Hartford
- E.D. #6
- Image 51 of 56

There's also a great selection of Mark Twain quotes at: *http://www.twainquotes.com/*

Cemetery Articles

Looking for more information on cemeteries? Check out these articles from Ancestry.com's free reference Library:

"How Not to Conduct a Cemetery Research Trip,"
by Linda Herrick Swisher (*Ancestry Daily News*, 20 July 2000)
http://www.ancestry.com/library/view/news/articles/2006.asp

"Buried in a Cemetery?" by Michael John Neill
(*Ancestry Daily News*, 27 June 2001)
http://www.ancestry.com/library/view/news/articles/4142.asp

"Carved in Stone: Clues in the Graveyard,"
by Karen Frisch
(*Ancestry* Magazine, September/October 2000, Vol. 18 No. 5)
http://www.ancestry.com/library/view/ancmag/2974.asp

More Cemetery Quick Tip Jamborees
(*Ancestry Daily News,* 12 July 2000)
http://www.ancestry.com/library/view/news/articles/1946.asp
(*Ancestry Daily News,* 28 June 2000)
http://www.ancestry.com/library/view/news/articles/1799.asp
(*Ancestry Daily News,* 16 May 2001)
http://www.ancestry.com/library/view/news/articles/3902.asp
(*Ancestry Daily News,* 30 October 2001)
http://www.ancestry.com/library/view/news/tip/4807.asp

"A Visit with a Cemetery Administrator,"
by George G. Morgan
("Along Those Lines . . ." 15 September 2000)
http://www.ancestry.com/library/view/news/articles/2326.asp

"Coincidence? Serendipitous Events at the Cemetery,"
by Christopher C. Bain
(*Ancestry* Magazine, September/October 2001 Vol. 19 No. 5)
http://www.ancestry.com/library/view/ancmag/4784.asp

"Cemetery Research Online,"
by George G. Morgan
("Along Those Lines . . ." 28 September 2001
http://www.ancestry.com/library/view/columns/george/4636.asp

"Aspen 2000 for Cemetery, Funeral Home, and Obituary Records,"
by Dick Eastman
("Eastman's Online Genealogy Newsletter," 26 Sept 2001)
http://www.ancestry.com/library/view/columns/eastman/4618.asp

If that's not enough, just go to <http://www.ancestry.com/learn/library/main.htm> and search for "cemetery."

Announcing Ancestry.Co.Uk!!
To expand its product offering beyond the borders of the United States, Ancestry.com recently launched a new subscription that caters to users in the United Kingdom and Ireland.

Acting as an extension of Ancestry.com, Ancestry.co.uk offers users access to seventy-five million records such as the Pallot Marriage and Baptismal Indexes, Parish and Probate Records, and the Civil Registration Index. In addition to the searchable databases, the site also provides localized content to help family historians with UKI-specific research issues. With the added convenience of a site specialized for the United Kingdom, Ancestry.co.uk is the ultimate resource for accelerating your family history research. Sign up today at:

<http://www.ancestry.com/rd/redir.asp?sourceid=1381&targetid=3575>

Looking for Past *Ancestry Daily News* articles? With the new site design, you can now find links to today's *Ancestry Daily News,* articles and to the Ancestry.com Library under the "Genealogy Help" button, or by clicking here: <http://www.ancestry.com/learn/main.htm>

User Comments at Ancestry.com

Ancestry.com now offers the ability to post "User Comments." Made available within all text databases at Ancestry.com, "User Comments" allows family history researchers to post brief comments or annotations to any text record on the Ancestry.com site.

This feature allows greater collaboration among the Ancestry.com user community by enabling researchers to connect with others sharing research interests, and allowing them to profit from the experience and efforts of previous researchers.

The tool, which was developed to emulate the successful "Postems" feature on RootsWeb.com, Ancestry's sister site, also allows genealogists to upload attachments as part of their comments. A comment regarding conflicting information in a record might include a scanned image as support material.

Often researchers uncover conflicting information in original records or source documentation created by errors from long ago. These errors and omissions may send family researchers in the wrong direction. "User Comments" allows those who have run into errors or obstacles to post this information, saving time and frustration for those who encounter these records later.

Additionally, researchers will be able to assist and aid others interested in the same records with their own insights or links to other files on Ancestry.com.

Advanced Search
http://www.ancestry.com/rd/advanced.htm

Subscribe to Ancestry.com and gain access to over 1.5 billion records at:
http://www.ancestry.com/rd/signup.htm

MyFamily.com and Family Reunions
Family reunions can take a lot of pre-planning and collaboration. MyFamily.com sites are ideal for outlining plans and collaborating with family members before the event. Online chats and news keep everyone in the loop and there's even a place to post family recipes and traditions that will make your reunion really special! Then afterwards, relive the event by sharing photos and stories on the site. Plan your reunion today at <http://www.myfamily.com>.
For more help on planning your family reunion, check out George G. Morgan's *Your Family Reunion: How to Plan It, Organize It, and Enjoy It*, at:
http://www.ancestry.com/rd/prodredir.asp?sourceid=831&key=P2460

How-to Help at Your Fingertips
The Ancestry.com Library makes available nearly 5,600 free articles and tips with the click of the mouse. Search articles from past issues of the *Ancestry Daily News, Ancestry* Magazine, *Genealogical Computing*, and "Dick Eastman's Online Genealogy Newsletter" at:
http://www.ancestry.com/learn/main.htm
(or by clicking "Genealogy Help" in the navigation bar at the top of any Ancestry.com page)

Memorial Day Articles in the Ancestry.com Library
"Military Records off the Beaten Path," by Curt B. Witcher
(*Ancestry* Magazine, Sep/Oct 2001, Vol. 19, No. 5)
http://www.ancestry.com/rd/prodredir.asp?sourceid=831&key=A478913

"World War I Draft Registration Cards," by Michael John Neill
("Beyond the Index," 26 December 2001)
http://www.ancestry.com/rd/prodredir.asp?sourceid=831&key=A505601

"World War II Draft Cards," by Michael John Neill
('Beyond the Index,' 27 March 2002)
http://www.ancestry.com/rd/prodredir.asp?sourceid=831&key=A547401

"Remembering World War II," by Heather Stratford
(*Ancestry* Magazine, May/June 2001, Vol. 19, No. 3)
http://www.ancestry.com/rd/prodredir.asp?sourceid=831&key=A415213

"Lest We Forget: The Value of Military Service Records,"
by Roseann Reinemuth Hogan, Ph.D.
(*Ancestry* Magazine, Mar/Apr 2000, Vol. 18, No. 2)
http://www.ancestry.com/rd/prodredir.asp?sourceid=831&key=A251013

"Family History Made Easy-Step 11: Military Records"
by Terry and Jim Willard
(*Ancestry* Magazine, Sept/Oct 2000, Vol. 18, No. 5)
http://www.ancestry.com/rd/prodredir.asp?sourceid=831&key=A298413

"Disguised Patriots: Women Who Served Incognito,"
by Elizabeth Kelley Kerstens, CGRS, CGL
(*Ancestry* Magazine, Mar/Apr 2000, Vol. 18, No. 2)
http://www.ancestry.com/rd/prodredir.asp?sourceid=831&key=A251313

"A Call to Arms, A Call to Honor," by Curt B. Witcher
(*Ancestry* Magazine, July/August 1999, vol. 19, no. 4)
http://www.ancestry.com/rd/prodredir.asp?sourceid=831&key=A019813

"Civil War Pension Records," by George G. Morgan
("Along Those Lines . . ." 18 December 1998)
http://www.ancestry.com/rd/prodredir.asp?sourceid=831&key=A093906

"Finding Your Patriot: Basic Sources for Starting Revolutionary War Research," by Curt B. Witcher
(*Ancestry* Magazine, May/June 1996, Vol. 14, No. 3)
http://www.ancestry.com/rd/prodredir.asp?sourceid=831&key=A215213

"Lost Soul," by Rebekah Thorstenson
(*Ancestry* Magazine, July/August 1999, vol. 19, no. 4)
http://www.ancestry.com/rd/prodredir.asp?sourceid=831&key=A020613

"In Search of the Graves of Our War Dead," by George G. Morgan
("Along Those Lines . . ." 16 June 2000)
http://www.ancestry.com/rd/prodredir.asp?sourceid=831&key=A159206

"Military Regimental Histories," by George G. Morgan
("Along Those Lines . . ." 2 July 1999)
http://www.ancestry.com/rd/prodredir.asp?sourceid=831&key=A087206

"Veterans in Your Family: Finding Background History and Images to Supplement Your Family History" by Juliana Smith
(*Ancestry Daily News* 11 November 1999)
http://www.ancestry.com/rd/prodredir.asp?sourceid=831&key=A047701

"Somewhere in France," by Juliana Smith
(*Ancestry* Magazine, January/February 1997, vol. 16, no. 1)
http://www.ancestry.com/rd/prodredir.asp?sourceid=831&key=A136413

Heirloom Family Trees
Ancestry.com Online Family Tree (OFT) users can create professional Heirloom Family Trees to put their family histories on display. Choose from a variety of backgrounds, sizes, styles, and frames, and Ancestry.com will mount and frame your Heirloom Family Tree. Details are available at:
http://www.ancestry.com/oft/hft/HFTLandPage.asp

Start your Online Family Tree at:
http://www.ancestry.com/oft

Find a Society at Society Hall

A quick and easy way to locate a society in your area of interest is at the Federation of Genealogical Societies (FGS) Society Hall. It's free and can be searched by location, keyword, or name. Societies can also add their information to the database by following quick and easy instructions. Visit Society Hall at:

<http://www.familyhistory.com/societyhall/main.asp>

Free Charts & Forms

You can download free charts and forms to help organize and record your family history at:

http://www.ancestry.com/save/charts/ancchart.htm
(Requires free Adobe Acrobat Reader)

Charts include:

- *Ancestral Chart*

  Allows you to record the ancestors from whom you directly descend.

- *Census Extraction*

  Allows you to record census information. Forms are available from 1790 to 1920.

- *Correspondence Record*

  Helps you keep track of those with whom you have corresponded.

- *Family Group Sheet*

  Enables you to compile complete, correct and connect families.

- *Research Calendar*

  Gives an account of every record source you have searched.

- *Research Extraction*

  Summarizes information that may be time-consuming or difficult to reread quickly.

- *Source Summary*

  Provides quick reference to information and sources you have found for a particular family.

Printing and Saving Census Images
By right-clicking on census images in Ancestry.com's Images Online, users that have downloaded the MrSID viewer can print and/or save the images to their hard drive.

Tips:
- When printing, you will get more of the image if you change the orientation to "landscape."
- Images can be saved as JPEG (.jpg), or Microsoft Bitmap (.bmp) and the portion of the image that is on the screen is what will be saved.

Five Reasons to Start Your Family Tree at Ancestry.com
We hope you enjoy using all of the features available at Ancestry.com to create, grow, save, and share your family tree. The following is a list of five reasons to use Ancestry.com as the center of your family history research:

1. Finds—You'll locate more information on your ancestors fast. Ancestry.com combines family tree functionality with actual databases. You can find information on your ancestors by searching more than 1.2 billion names directly from the Online Family Tree.

2. Sharing—You can share your tree with others privately or publicly. Submitting your tree to the Ancestry World Tree allows you to share your tree to genealogists all over the world. The Ancestry World Tree, which contains over 200 million names (including 25 million UK & Ireland names), is the largest database of its kind on the Internet.

3. Collaboration—Ancestry has a large community of dedicated researchers who help each other in their attempts to grow their family trees. The Online Family Tree also lets you invite others to participate in updating your family tree in a private, secure environment.

4. Ownership—You always own your data on Ancestry. Ancestry allows you to update or delete your family tree at any time. You will never find your data included on CD-ROMs or sold on Ancestry.

5. Helping others—When you share and collaborate with others on your tree, you will also be helping others with their research. You may have a specific date or event in your tree that someone else has been trying to find for years.

Download free Ancestry Family Tree software at:
<http://aft.ancestry.com>

Or start your free Online Family Tree at:
<http://www.ancestry.com/oft>

Index

New York *(cont.)*
Family History Library, 41
Historical and Genealogical Miscellany: New York and New Jersey, 104-108
Manhattan New York City Directory (1829-30), 112
New York Births and Baptisms: Schohaire and Mohawk Valleys, 115-116
1920 U.S. Census Indexes, 126-127
Records of the Town of East Hampton, Long Island, Suffolk County, New York, 117-118
The Source, 41
USGenWeb website for, 40
New York Times, website for, 135
News and Announcements
Allen County Library research, 157-158
Ancestry.com price increase, 152-153, 158
Ancestry.com redesign, 150-151
California records access hearing, 151-152
computer virus, 152
Federation of Genealogical Societies resolution, 154-157
National Archives new website design, 159-160
1920 Census completion, 153-154, 158

Newspaper collections
Fort Wayne News, 134
Fort Wayne Sentinel, 134-135
Nevada State Journal, 135

New York Times, 135
Reno Weekly Gazette and *Stockman* (1889-99), 136
searching of, 133
Nicodemus, Charles, 139
North Carolina, 1920 U.S. Census Indexes, 126-127
North Dakota, 1920 U.S. Census Indexes, 126-127

O
Occupational records, Brunswick and Topsham Village, Maine City Directory (1910), 98-99
Ohio, 1920 U.S. Census Indexes, 126-127
Oklahoma, 1920 U.S. Census Indexes, 126-127
Oregon, 1920 U.S. Census Indexes, 126-127
O'Rell, Max, 144

P
Pallot's Index
advanced searches, 79
beginnings of, 78
contents of, 78-79
result displays, 83
search techniques for, 81-8
searching ease of, 79
shortcomings of, 79-80
web access to, 80
Pennsylvania, 1920 U.S. Census Indexes, 126-127
Personal Digital Assistants (PDAs)
functions on, 48-50
genealogy use on, 50-51
possibilities of, 51
types of, 48

Rhode Island *(cont.)*
  1930 U.S. Census Images and
    Indexes, 125
  1920 U.S. Census Indexes, 126-
    127
RootsWeb, mailing list of, 16
Rothschild, Charles J., 144
Royal Irish Constabulary, database
  for, 185
Ryan, Tim, 146

S
Safety, cell phone use, 162-163
Sargent, Ida, 29-32
Scottish records
  Scotch-Irish: The Scot in North
    Britain, North Ireland, and
    North America, 119-120
  See also United Kingdom data-
    bases
Society Hall, resources on, 193
Soundex
  name searching, 171
  searching on, 4
The Source, state census records in, 41
South Dakota, 1920 U.S. Census
  Indexes, 126-127
Stinchcomb, Frank, 137
Stinchcomb, Shaw, 137

T
Tennessee, 1920 U.S. Census
  Indexes, 126-127
Texas, 1920 U.S. Census Indexes,
  126-127

U
United Kingdom databases
  Ancestry subscription for, 188-
    189

Burke's Commons of Great
  Britain and Ireland, 128
Cheshire, England: Parish and
  Probate Records, 128-129
Suffolk, England: Parish and
  Probate Records, 129-130
Yorkshire, England: Parish and
  Probate Records, 130-131
See also Irish databases, Scottish
  records
Utah
  1930 U.S. Census Images and
    Indexes, 125
  1920 U.S. Census Indexes, 126-
    127

V
Vermont
  1930 U.S. Census Images and
    Indexes, 125
  1920 U.S. Census Indexes, 126-
    127
Virginia
  1920 U.S. Census Indexes, 126-
    127
  Virginia County Records, 120-
    121

W
War letters
  books publishing of, 90
  Legacy Project and, 90
  preservation efforts, 87-90
Warrington, Carrie C., 144
Washington, 1920 U.S. Census
  Indexes, 126-127
West Virginia, 1920 U.S. Census
  Indexes, 126-127
Wills
  Calendar of Delaware Wills,